A PRACTICAL GUIDE TO LIFE'S ESSENTIAL DAILY HABIT

# I Heard GOD Laugh

## MATTHEW KELLY

**BLUE SPARROW**
North Palm Beach, Florida

BLUE
sparrow

Copyright © 2020
KAKADU, LLC
PUBLISHED BY BLUE SPARROW

ISBN: 978-1-63582-138-3 (hardcover)
ISBN: 978-1-63582-139-0 (e-book)

*Designed by* Ashley Wirfel

10   9   8   7   6   5   4   3   2

FIRST EDITION

Printed in the United States of America

Nothing will change your life so completely, absolutely, and forever like really learning how to pray.

# Table of Contents

# PART ONE

## The Unexpected Life

IS YOUR LIFE unfolding the way you thought it would? I was paging through my high school yearbook recently. There were 161 young men in my graduating class, and fewer than a handful are doing what they thought, hoped, or dreamed they would be doing. Most of them are glad. When they were seventeen or eighteen, they didn't know themselves well enough to decide what they were going to do for the rest of their lives. And that's just work and career.

Life doesn't turn out the way we expect. In some ways it exceeds our expectations, and in other ways it disappoints them. There may be hopes and dreams that were part of the life we expected that we need to grieve because they didn't materialize. But there are also hopes and dreams we had when we were younger that we are glad did not come to be.

We see now that we were ill-suited for them, and they were ill-suited for us. At the same time, there are things about the unexpected life that surprise and delight.

Life doesn't unfold as we plan. We all live unexpected lives in one way or another. But sooner or later, we have to decide how we are going to make the most of the unexpected life. It is then that we come face-to-face with two enduring truths: We cannot live without the hope that things will change for the better, and we are not victims of our circumstances.

You are not what has happened to you. You are not what you have accomplished. You are not even who you are today or who you have become so far. You are also who and what you are still capable of becoming. You are your realized and unrealized potential. God sees you and all your potential, and he aches to see you embrace your best, truest, highest self. He yearns to help you and to accompany you in that quest.

Wherever you are, whatever you're feeling, however life has surprised and disappointed you, I want to remind you of one thing: The best is yet to come! There are times in life when this is easier or harder to believe, but the best is truly yet to come. Open yourself up to it, so you can see it and embrace it when it emerges!

## A QUESTION TO BEGIN

Is your life working? It's a simple question, really. We cannot look at another person's life and know, but most of the time, we know how well our own life is (or isn't) working.

When we reflect upon our lives, we usually discover that in some ways they are functioning well and in other ways they are dysfunctional. What does this mean for you? It means in some ways you are flourishing, but in other ways you are experiencing dissatisfaction. God is speaking to you through that dissatisfaction. You can learn to live with your discontent, or you can accept it as an invitation.

The danger zone is marked by comfort. This is where things aren't great, but they aren't horrible either, so you just continue to muddle along. We gravitate toward comfort, and it's amazing how comfortable we can get with things that are uncomfortable or worse. The thought of something new and unknown activates our resistance and hesitancy. These are mental, emotional, and spiritual obstacles that we all need to push through in order to move from surviving to thriving. Are you thriving or just surviving? It's time to stop muddling along.

If your life isn't working, what are you willing to do about it? Are you open to trying something new? This book is an invitation to flourish and thrive like never before.

## THE MISSING PIECE

Trying to put together a jigsaw puzzle without an important piece is incredibly frustrating. That is the story of millions of people's lives. Day after day they are frustrated, but they don't realize they are missing a piece. They drive themselves crazy trying to put the puzzle of their own lives together without that critical piece.

The essential piece most people are missing is a vibrant spirituality.

You're a human being, a delicate composition of body and soul, mysteriously linked by the will and the intellect. The important word here is *soul*. You have a soul. It is literally your life force. When it leaves your body, you die.

It's time to start paying more attention to your soul. Think about these four aspects of the human person: body, soul, will, intellect. We are obsessed with three of them: body, will, and intellect. We pamper our bodies, vigorously defend our right to decide the path we walk, and celebrate our individual and collective intellectual accomplishments. Yet, we often ignore the most important, soul. Have you been taking care of your soul? Rate yourself between one and ten. Most of us neglect the soul in favor of the body. The body is constantly barking orders at us: Feed me, wash me, clothe me, pleasure me, feed me again, and so on. The body makes a continuous stream of demands upon us. The soul, on the other hand, is quiet and faithful. When the soul is hungry, our stomach doesn't rumble and growl. But it is important to feed our soul each day.

Yes, each day. How many days has it been since you intentionally fed your soul? You are a spiritual being having a physical experience in this world. You have a soul. Feeding your soul is the missing piece of the puzzle. There is no better time than right now to nurture your inner life, discover your spiritual needs, and feed your soul.

It is time to stop ignoring our souls. The soul integrates and harmonizes every aspect of our humanity. It re-orients us toward what matters most.

## THE HABIT

There are an unlimited number of ways to feed your soul. The best place to start is with daily prayer. It is the cornerstone of the spiritual life. Sometimes people will argue and assert that going to church on Sunday is the cornerstone of the spiritual life. But there are tens of millions of people who go to church every Sunday but do not have a vibrant spiritual life.

The habit of daily prayer may not sound exciting to you. If you feel that way, it's because you haven't experienced daily prayer in the ways we are going to discuss in this book. And there is a very clear reason for that. The most astounding thing I have discovered in my quest to help people grow spiritually is that most have never been taught how to pray. Many of us learned to say prayers as children, but there is a whole spiritual world that most people have never experienced. It is a world most have never even been introduced to.

So, let me ask you a question: Has anyone ever taught you how to pray? If your answer is no or "Not really" or "I'm not sure," today is going to be one of the most memorable days of your life.

Don't get me wrong, it is disappointing and sad and tragic that so many of us can make our way so far through life without being taught how to really pray. But it also means that so many amazing possibilities are still undiscovered before you. It means the best is definitely yet to come.

Nothing will change your life so completely, absolutely, and forever like learning how to really pray. In prayer we learn who we are and what we are here for, what matters most and what matters least. Through prayer we discover the-best-version-of-ourselves, and are given the courage to celebrate and defend it in each moment of each day. In prayer we learn how to love and be loved, because we discover that we have been loved, are loved, and will continually be loved by God.

It is an unavoidable fact that our lives do not unfold as we hope and expect them to. It is also worth pointing out that very often we are defined by how we respond to the unexpected events of life. The unexpected, whether good or bad, reveals character. How then do we prepare for the un-expected? Prayer. Prayer is the ultimate preparation for the unexpected. Prayer helps us develop the awareness, virtue, and character that are essential when your life gets turned upside down.

There is a storm coming. How do I know? There always is. It may be days away, weeks or months, or even years. But it is coming. Nobody passes through this life without encountering some storms. A tornado blew through our neighborhood a few nights ago. The next day seventy thousand households had no electricity, and hundreds of trees had been torn down. Other trees looked untouched. What is the difference between two trees, side by side, one gets blown to the ground and the other continues to stand tall? Strong roots. A tree with strong roots can weather almost any storm. A tree with deep roots bears great fruit, for it can source the water and nutrients it needs from the earth.

Sink the roots of the daily habit of prayer deep into your life. Is there a storm coming? Life has taught me that this is the wrong question. When will the storm get here? is more appropriate. Life has also taught me that when the storm arrives it is too late to start sinking those roots. So, don't delay. Begin today.

Prayer is life's essential daily habit.

## THE PROMISE OF THIS BOOK

This book is about that habit of prayer. Every book makes a promise. Sometimes that promise is stated clearly as the goal or objective of the book, but often it is not. Whenever I set out to write a new book, I like to get very clear before I begin about the promise I am making to you, the reader. The promise of this book is that it will teach you how to pray and introduce you to a world of spirituality that most people have never experienced. I specifically want to teach you a form a prayer that will help you develop a vibrant habit of daily prayer. Some books find us at just the right time, and they change our lives forever. I believe that if I can fulfill the promise of this book, it may become one of those books for you and many others.

There is a difference between knowing about a person and knowing a person, and it's an enormous difference. There is also a difference between knowing about prayer and experiencing prayer. Our aim here is not to know everything there is to know about prayer. We are striving to have a powerful experience of prayer.

My goal at every turn is to help you develop a dynamic habit of daily prayer. For these reasons, this book is in no way supposed to be a treatise on prayer, but rather a short, practical, hopeful guide designed to help you have a powerful experience of prayer.

My greatest hope is that you return to this book time and

time again, like a touchstone, a trusted companion for your onward spiritual journey.

## FINDING YOUR REASON

You may be asking: Why should I pray? It's a great question. It is also the answer. We have so many questions, and all too often we turn to the people around us as we look for answers, instead of turning to the one who has all the answers to all the questions. Your questions are the gateway to the answers you seek. Treasure your questions. Honor them enough to seek answers, and not just any answers. My sense is that you are not looking for generalized answers quoted to you from a book. You yearn for deeply personal answers to your deeply personal questions. The world cannot give you these. The people in your life cannot answer these questions for you, even those who know you and love you most. If you truly want to seek and find these answers, this is work for the soul. These are matters that are between you and God.

Why should you pray? Instead of giving you all the standard theological answers and reasons, I think it is more important for you to find your own reasons.

My own reasons have evolved over time. In the beginning, my reasons for praying each day were not elevated theological reasons; they were simple and practical. When

I spent a few minutes in prayer in the morning, I seemed to have a better day than when I didn't; I had more clarity when I was making decisions, and I experienced a peace that I had never known until I started praying each day. I encourage you to observe these things in yourself as you begin to practice prayer in the ways I describe as this book unfolds.

Questions play an important role in our spiritual journey, and I urge you to jot down and date the questions you have along the way. You will look back at different times; these questions and the dates you began asking them will provide powerful context to your journey. They will show where you have been and encourage you in where you are going.

The essential practical virtue of prayer is patience—which is also the essential practical virtue in all relationships. This is our first encounter with a truth that will surface time and time again: Prayer teaches us how to live and love. Prayer teaches us to be patient, and two patient people will always have a better relationship than two impatient people. There is also a direct connection between our capacity to love and our capacity for patience. Perhaps this is why, when describing what love is in 1 Corinthians 13, Paul begins, "Love is patient . . ."

At the beginning of a journey, it is natural to be excited and a little impatient, but I beg you, take it in, look around, breathe it all in, and drink fully this experience. In a letter to a friend, the poet Rainer Maria Rilke wrote, "Be patient toward all that is unsolved in your heart and try to love the questions themselves, like locked rooms and like books that are now written in a very foreign tongue. Do not now seek the answers, which cannot be given you because you would not be able to live them. And the point is, to live everything. Live the questions now. Perhaps you will then gradually, without noticing it, live along some distant day into the answer."

It takes courage to place our questions before God in prayer. It takes patience to wait for the answers, which are sometimes given to us in prayer and sometimes delivered through other people and the experience of daily life. It takes wisdom to live the answers we discover. I pray you are blessed with an abundance of courage, patience, and wisdom for the journey we are embarking upon.

I am often asked: "Why do you pray?" I pray because I cannot thrive without it.

There is a much-quoted statement by Henry David Thoreau that reads, "Most men lead lives of quiet desperation." Thoreau was determined not to live such a life himself, and so, at the age of twenty-seven, he went off into the woods to live alone and reflect upon life. He remained there at Walden Pond for two years and two months. His life and writings continue to inspire millions of people to live more deliberately today. Writing about his reasons for the Walden experiment, Thoreau observed, "I went to the woods because I wanted to live deliberately. . . . I wanted to live deep and suck out all the marrow of life . . . to put aside all that was not life, and not, when I came to die, discover that I had not lived."

I pray for many of the same reasons. I go to the woods of prayer each day because I want to live life deliberately. I pray because I want to live my one short life intentionally and deeply. I go to prayer to learn what matters most and what doesn't matter at all, to separate those things that are important from those that are of little or no consequence. I pray because I love how prayer rearranges my priorities. I go to the woods of prayer because I do not want to come to die and discover that I have not lived.

Why do I pray? My many reasons are constantly changing and evolving. But perhaps the most consistent and transparent reasons are: I cannot live without prayer. I don't know how people remain sane or even survive in this crazy, noisy, busy world without it. But more than that, I pray because I don't wish to live without it. I cannot imagine life without prayer. I have lived with and without it, and I never wish to go back to a prayerless life. I have known prayerfulness and I have known prayerlessness. My commitment to prayer has not always been as consistent as I would have liked, but I have no desire to go back to the disillusionment of prayerlessness.

But these are my reasons, and you will discover your own. For now, I ask you to consider this: Could pausing to take a few minutes with God each day change everything for the

better? And yes, I mean everything. Is it possible?
I assure you, it is.

## HABIT AND POTENTIAL

Our lives change when our habits change. For better or for
worse, habits are one of the most powerful influences in
our lives. Our lives rise and fall more on our habits than on
circumstances beyond our control. There is so much uncertainty in life, so much that is beyond our circle of influence, but with our habits we get to exercise our God-given
free will and shape our destiny.

Earlier, we briefly discussed the idea of your past and
your potential. You are not what has happened to you. You
are not your accomplishments. You are not even who you
are today or who you have become so far. You are who and
what you are still capable of becoming. You are your realized and unrealized potential. God sees you and all your
potential, and he aches to see you embrace your best, truest,
highest self. He yearns to help you and accompany you in
that quest.

Philosophers speak of "being." Anything that exists is a
being. Birds, fish, and dogs are all beings. Angels are beings.
God is a being. You are a being. There are different types of
beings. You are not God, or an angel, or a dog; you are a human being. One of the most amazing things about human

beings is that incredible changes can take place within us. Your being is not fixed, stagnant, or static; it is changeable. This is a beautiful thing, primarily because from it springs endless hope.

Here is something worth pondering: The being of something changeable—you—is not only what it is, but what it still can be. You are not only who and what you are today; your essence or being also includes who you are capable of becoming—who you still can be. I love this idea. It expresses the basis for hope in our potential, and potential is a beautiful thing. We see endless potential in small children and young people, but at some point we stop talking about it. This also probably means we stop thinking about our own potential.

"I am who I am," some people say. But this is a half-truth. You are who you are, but you are also who you are capable of becoming—and you have amazing potential. You may not see it. You may feel stuck or trapped, and you may be right now. But you do not have to stay stuck or trapped. God and your potential are ready to pull you out of all that with this new habit of daily prayer. Our potential is unleashed with new habits. Habits unlock our potential, and no habit does this like daily prayer. And this is only one of many qualities that make it life's essential daily habit.

Often when we speak of forming new habits, our motive is to look better, be more productive and efficient, accomplish more, and so on. In adopting a habit of daily prayer, these outcomes are not our goal, but you will achieve them indirectly. Peace is one of the fruits of daily prayer, and so few people have it that as you develop it, you begin to look different. A peaceful glow begins to emerge from you, and your eyes light up like never before. You will also be more efficient and accomplish more, because as you see clearly what matters most and what matters least, you prioritize your time and energy to achieve better outcomes.

Habits are incredibly powerful. They reach into every corner of our lives. This is more true for the habit of daily prayer than perhaps for any other habit.

## THE CHALLENGE

In this book I am going to teach you a life-changing method of prayer. I know it is life-changing because it changed my life and has changed the lives of countless men, women, and children of all ages.

It takes twenty-one days to establish a new habit in our lives, to sink its roots sufficiently so that the first strong breeze doesn't blow it away. I challenge you to spend just ten minutes at the beginning of each of the next twenty-one days practicing the method of prayer we are about to explore.

Throughout these twenty-one days, I invite you to reflect upon and take note of all the ways beginning your day with prayer has changed you and your life. Ask yourself: Are my days different? How? Do I feel different? Is my mood different? Do I treat people the same as before? Am I a better husband, wife, mother, father, son, daughter, sister, brother, friend, colleague, neighbor? In what ways has beginning each day with prayer improved my life?

I am a practical man. So if you are still hesitant to commit, think of all the other ways you have tried to find fulfillment and happiness in this life. What do you have to lose? The most you can lose is a few minutes each day for a few weeks. What do you have to gain? The upside is unfathomable.

Ten minutes a day for twenty-one days. Give it a try. For my part, I promise to teach you and encourage you, to give you all the tools you need to fulfill this commitment.

## SOUL NOTE:

*Soul,*
*You have the heart of a lion, strong and courageous.*
*Let nothing distract you, let nobody discourage you*
*from your daily communion with the one who created you.*

# PART TWO

# My Spiritual Journey

MY SPIRITUAL ODYSSEY began in earnest when I was fifteen years old. I didn't know it at the time, but it was the beginning of a conversion experience. The word *conversion* is often used when someone changes from one religion to another. I converted from secular consumerism. I had been raised in the faith, but it had never really taken root in my heart and life.

The most famous conversion story in history is that of Paul. He spent his life hunting Christians, until he was knocked to the ground on the road to Damascus and God spoke to him. Was it a moment of transformation? Yes. Was it his only moment of transformation? No. For the rest of his life he strived and struggled to embrace the teachings of Jesus.

We often think of a conversion as a single decision or event, when the reality is that we are called to continuous conversion. The experience I am about to describe that took place when I was fifteen was the beginning of a process of conversion—a transformation—that continues to this day. Some people have a conversion experience because they encounter tragedy and grasp for God to survive the brutal stroke that life has struck. Others experience conversion because things are going well but still they sense that something is missing. This is where I was when God woke me up from my aimless wandering.

## THE INVITATION: TEN MINUTES A DAY

At the time, I was in high school. Everything at school was going very well—I had a great group of friends and a wonderful girlfriend, I was doing well in my studies, I played on a number of sports teams, and I had a good part-time job. On the outside everything seemed fine, but on the inside a certain restlessness was building up. My heart was restless. I sensed that something was missing in my life. I knew something was wrong, but I couldn't pinpoint it. I just had a nagging feeling that there must be more to life, but I didn't know what it was or where to find it. For too long I tried to ignore these feelings, but the restlessness persisted.

Several weeks later I bumped into a family friend and he

asked me how school was going. "Fine," I told him. He was a doctor, so he knew how to ask the right questions, and for five or ten minutes he gently probed the different areas of my life. Each question and answer led us a little closer to his diagnosis. Then he paused briefly, looked deep into my eyes, and said, "You're not really happy, are you, Matthew?" He knew it and I knew it, but I was ashamed to admit it at first. But our lives seem to flood with grace at unexpected moments, and I began to tell him about the emptiness and restlessness I was experiencing.

After listening to me carefully, he suggested I stop by church for ten minutes each morning on the way to school. I listened, smiled, nodded politely, and immediately dismissed him as some sort of religious fanatic. As he expanded on his idea and how it would transform my life, I wondered to myself, "How is ten minutes of prayer each day going to help me?" Before he had finished speaking, I had resolved to completely ignore everything he said.

In the coming weeks, I threw myself into my studies, my work, and my sporting pursuits with more vigor than ever before. I had done this to appease my restless heart at other times in my life. But achievement in these areas no longer brought the fulfillment it once had.

## THE FIRST SURRENDER

One morning about six weeks later, the emptiness had become so great that I found myself stopping by the church on the way to school. I crept quietly in, sat near the back, and began to plan my day. Just planning the day ahead of me lifted the clouds of hurried confusion. For the first time in my life I tasted a few drops of that wonderful tonic we call peace—and I liked it.

The next day, and every day after that, I returned. Each morning I would sit toward the back of the church and simply move through the events of the day in my mind. With each passing day a sense of peace, purpose, and direction began to fill me.

Then one day as I sat there it occurred to me that planning my day wasn't really prayer. So I began to pray: "God, I want this . . . and I need this . . . and could you do this for me . . . and help me with this . . . and let this happen . . . and please, don't let that happen . . ."

It continued this way for a few weeks. Every morning I would stop by church, sit toward the back, plan my day, and give God his instructions for the day. Of course, at the time I didn't realize the arrogance and irony of that.

For a while this was the depth of my prayer life. And then one day I had a problem. That morning I stopped by church, and with a simple prayer in my heart, I said to God, "God, I've got this problem. . . . This is the situation. . . . These are the circumstances. . . ." Then I stumbled onto the question that would change my life forever: "God, what do you think I should do?"

With that question my life began to change. Asking that question marked a new beginning in my life. Up until then, I had only ever prayed, "Listen up, God, your servant is speaking." But in that moment of spontaneous prayer, the Spirit that guides us all led me to pray, "Speak, Lord, your servant is listening." It was perhaps the first moment of honest and humble prayer in my life. Before that day, I had only been interested in telling God what *my* will was. Now for the first time I was asking God to reveal his will.

*God, what do you think I should do?* I call this the Big Question. It is the question that changed my life forever, and it continues to transform my life on a daily basis when I have the courage to ask it. This question should be a constant theme in our spiritual lives. When we are attentive to it, we find a joy that is independent of external realities, because we have a peace and contentment within. It is the peace that comes from knowing that who we are and what we are doing makes sense, regardless of the outcome and regardless of other people's opinions. This peace comes from elevating the only opinion that truly matters: God's.

Our choices are the foundation of our lives. Every day we make dozens of decisions, some of them large and some of them small. When was the last time you invited God into the decisions of your life?

I *try* each day to let God play a role in my decision making, but often the allure of this world distracts me. Sometimes I simply forget to consult him. Sometimes I block his voice out because I want to do something that isn't good for me. Sometimes I foolishly believe that I know a shortcut to happiness. These decisions always lead me to misery in one form or another.

There is one question that consistently leads to lasting happiness in this changing world: *God, what do you think I should do?* To think we can find happiness without asking this question is one of our grandest delusions. This question has led men and women from all walks of life to discover who they are and what they are here for. Now it is your turn.

## THE DAY MY LIFE CHANGED FOREVER

There is a gratitude that is so great it is inexpressible, a gratitude that goes on and on. That is the kind of gratitude I have for John, the man who first challenged and encouraged me to pray. For thirty years, I have been telling the story I just shared with you. I share it in hopes that it will encourage others to adopt the life-changing habit of daily prayer. But recently as I reflected on my journey, I came to realize that I have been leaving out an essential piece of the story. As I share that with you now, I think you will gain a clearer sense of my gratitude for this man.

Until this point in the story, I had been praying each day for several months, but I really had no idea what I was doing. Looking back now, I realize I was fumbling and stumbling around in the dark. Knowing what I know today, it seems like a miracle that I persevered. But then something else happened.

I asked you earlier if anyone has ever taught you how to pray. Nobody had ever taught me. As a child I had been taught to say prayers, I had been encouraged to pray, and I had heard people talk about the importance of prayer, but I had not been taught *how* to pray. That was all about to change.

This is how it happened.

On our way to play basketball one day, John and I were driving past a church, when he said to me, "Have you done your ten minutes today?" I told him I had. "This is a spectacularly beautiful church," he continued. "Why don't we make a visit and spend a few minutes in prayer?"

As we were walking toward the church John said, "Let's try something different today. When we sit down, I will say a brief opening prayer, and then I would like to read some short passages from the Bible. I will read them one at a time. After I read each passage, I'd like to encourage you to have a conversation with God about whatever those few lines say to you. I will do the same. The passages may inspire you and encourage you; others may challenge you.

It doesn't matter. Just talk to God about whatever he places on your heart. After two or three minutes, I will read another short passage."

We walked into the church and sat toward the front. It was the middle of the afternoon and the church was completely empty. After a moment, he began, "My Lord and my God, we thank you for all the ways you have blessed us in the past, all the ways you are blessing us today, and all the ways you plan to bless us in the future. Open our hearts and minds to the wisdom you desire to share with us during this time of prayer. Amen." Then we sat there for a moment; I could tell he was giving us a chance to settle into the experience.

Then he read the following passage from the Bible, and we each spoke to God in our hearts about what we heard.

"Seeing the crowds, he went up on the mountain, and when he sat down his disciples came to him. And he opened his mouth and taught them, saying: Blessed are the poor in spirit, for theirs is the kingdom of heaven. Blessed are those who mourn, for they shall be comforted. Blessed are the meek, for they shall inherit the earth. Blessed are those who hunger and thirst for righteousness, for they shall be satisfied. Blessed are the merciful, for they shall obtain mercy. Blessed are the pure in heart, for they shall see God. Blessed are the peacemakers, for they shall be called sons of God. Blessed are those who are persecuted for righteousness' sake, for theirs is the kingdom of heaven. Blessed are you when men revile you and persecute you and utter all kinds of evil against you falsely on my account. Rejoice and be glad, for your reward is great in heaven, for so men persecuted the prophets who were before you." (Matthew 5:1–12)

I had heard the passage many times before at church and in school, but it struck me in ways it never had before. Each line inspired ideas and reflections. It was like trying to drink from a fire hydrant.

John paused in silence for about three minutes while I spoke to Jesus in my heart about what the passage was saying to me, how it challenged me, how it encouraged me, and how it convicted me. I was still in the midst of that conversation when John began reading the next passage.

"You are the salt of the earth; but if salt has lost its taste, how shall its saltiness be restored? It is no longer good for anything except to be thrown out and trodden under foot by men. You are the light of the world. A city set on a hill cannot be hid. Nor do men light a lamp and put it under a bushel, but on a stand, and it gives light to all in the house. Let your light so shine before men, that they may see your good works and give glory to your Father who is in heaven." (Matthew 5:13–16)

My high school motto—*Luceat Lux Vestra*, or "Let your light shine"—was drawn from this passage. My heart immediately gravitated toward that line. Was I letting my light shine? I spoke to Jesus about the ways I was and was not letting my light shine. And again, John began to read another passage.

"Therefore I tell you, do not be anxious about your life, what you shall eat or what you shall drink, nor about your body, what you shall put on. Is not life more than food, and the body more than clothing? Look at the birds of the air: they neither sow nor reap nor gather into barns, and yet your heavenly Father feeds them. Are you not of more value than they? And which of you by being anxious can add one cubit to his span of life? And why are you anxious about clothing? Consider the lilies of the field, how they grow; they neither toil nor spin; yet I tell you, even Solomon in all his glory was not arrayed like one of these. But if God so clothes the grass of the field, which today is alive and tomorrow is thrown into the oven, will he not much more clothe you, O men of little faith? Therefore do not be anxious, saying, 'What shall we eat?' or 'What shall we drink?' or 'What shall we wear?' For the Gentiles seek all these things; and your heavenly Father knows that you need them all. But seek first his kingdom and his righteousness, and all these things shall be yours as well. Therefore do not be anxious about tomorrow, for tomorrow will be anxious for itself. Let the day's own trouble be sufficient for the day." (Matthew 6:25–34)

Listening to this passage was like watching fireworks go off in my mind. I have always been a planner, and with that goes a certain amount of worry and anxiety. This passage challenged me then and it challenges me still today. I remember talking to Jesus and saying, "Lord, I think I believe, I want to believe. But I am struggling to turn things over to you and trust that everything will be OK." I got a very strong message in return, not in words, but he placed this idea in my heart: When God invites us to trust in him, he promises that everything will work out in the end, but he doesn't promise that everything will work out the way we want it to.

"Judge not, that you be not judged. For with the judgment you pronounce you will be judged, and the measure you give will be the measure you get. Why do you see the speck that is in your brother's eye, but do not notice the log that is in your own eye? Or how can you say to your brother, 'Let me take the speck out of your eye,' when there is the log in your own eye? You hypocrite, first take the log out of your own eye, and then you will see clearly to take the speck out of your brother's eye." (Matthew 7:1–5)

It is so easy to judge others. I remember thinking that. I remember being ashamed of how judgmental I was of other people. I remember asking God to take away all the judgment in my heart. And I remember sitting there wanting John to start reading the next passage, and after what seemed like an eternity, he did.

"Ask, and it will be given you; seek, and you will find; knock, and it will be opened to you. For every one who asks receives, and he who seeks finds, and to him who knocks it will be opened. Or what man of you, if his son asks him for bread, will give him a stone? Or if he asks for a fish, will give him a serpent? If you then, who are evil, know how to give good gifts to your children, how much more will your Father who is in heaven give good things to those who ask him! So whatever you wish that men would do to you, do so to them; for this is the law and the prophets." (Matthew 7:7–12)

My dad's business was struggling at the time, and I asked God to take away his stress and anxiety. I could see it was causing tension between my mother and my father, and I asked God to ease that tension.

"You will know them by their fruits. Are grapes gathered from thorns, or figs from thistles? So, every sound tree bears good fruit, but the bad tree bears evil fruit. A sound tree cannot bear evil fruit, nor can a bad tree bear good fruit. Every tree that does not bear good fruit is cut down and thrown into the fire. Thus you will know them by their fruits." (Matthew 7:16–20)

I wanted to bear good fruit. I didn't know how that could happen, but I had the desire. For the first time, I sat there not knowing what to say to God, but I had the sense that the desire to bear good fruit was itself a good start.

A few moments later, John prayed, "My Lord and My God, we thank you for these moments of prayer, and for all the inspirations and resolutions you have placed in our hearts. Give us the courage to live them in our lives. Amen."

Then he stood up, I stood up, and we walked back to the car. I didn't realize it at the time, but my life had just changed significantly and forever. What had happened? This man had taught me how to pray. It seems so simple and natural: He taught me how to pray. But it is rare. Most people have never been taught how to talk to God.

I thought we had been in the church for about fifteen minutes, but as we got back into the car the clock caught my eye; I discovered we had been in there for at least thirty minutes.

It was one of the most powerful experiences of my life. It wasn't someone talking about prayer or telling me to pray, and it wasn't someone talking to me about how to pray. It was someone actually *teaching* me how to pray. It took just a few minutes, but it changed my life forever.

This conversation with God about anything and everything that's happening in your life, about the things that are troubling you and the things that are bringing you joy, is at the heart of the spiritual life.

This method of prayer is sometimes referred to as mental prayer or contemplative prayer. I think of it simply as prayer of the heart—your heart speaking to God about whatever emerges in your soul. It is the prayer of conversation that the great saints and mystics practiced. But they would be the first to say it should be the way you and I pray also.

# MY HOPE FOR YOU

I didn't know it at the time, but the day I was taught how to pray was one of the best days of my life. Later I realized that John had probably planned that experience. I remember wondering why we were leaving so early when he first mentioned what time he would pick me up that day. But what a beautiful thing to plan. What an amazing gift.

All the passages he read that day were from the Gospel of Matthew. The following week, I asked him to write down the references, so I could reflect on them again. And over the years I have reflected on these exact passages many, many times.

I wish I could take you to your local church, sit next to you, and give you exactly the same experience that I was given. I hope this book will give you the tools and the confidence to practice this form of prayer yourself. And at some point in your journey, if you feel so called, I hope you will teach other people in your life how to pray in this way. You will be giving them an unimaginable gift.

There is nothing quite like a spiritual awakening. The sky seems bluer, the water tastes fresher, all of life appears in high definition, and every sight, sound, touch, and taste is richer and fuller. And it all begins with prayer.

Over the past thirty years, daily prayer has become one of the foundational habits of my life. It is my hope that it will soon become one of the foundational habits of your life too.

## SOUL NOTE:

*Soul,*
*Set the worries of this world aside,*
*and allow yourself to soar like a bird on the wind.*
*Listen to the whispers of your Creator calling gently to you,*
*inviting you to remember that just as the body needs food,*
*so too your soul needs to be nourished.*

# PART THREE

# Life's Essential Habit

OUR LIVES CHANGE when our habits change. They change for the better with good habits and for the worse with self-destructive habits. Daily prayer is life's essential habit, laying a foundation upon which many other great practical and spiritual habits can spring from.

## TEACH US TO PRAY

If you could ask God for anything, what would you choose? Solomon was just twelve years old when he became the King of Israel. Imagine becoming the leader of a great nation at such a young age. He was anxious about his ability to lead the nation, concerned about all the decisions he would need to make. Then, one night, God appeared to him in a dream. He told Solomon he would give him anything he asked for. What did Solomon request of God? He asked for wisdom.

The disciples traveled with Jesus for three years, witnessing him teach and heal, conversing with him as they walked along the dusty roads of Galilee. People were always trying to get close to Jesus to ask him for favors, but the disciples were right there—they could have asked for anything they wanted at any time. What did they ask for? They asked Jesus to teach them to pray.

They had seen Jesus go to quiet places to pray. We read about him going to a place set apart from everyone and everything else many times in the Gospels. It was clearly a habit for Jesus. In a way their request was the same as Solomon's; prayer is a pathway to wisdom.

The need and desire for prayer is universal. Often we are unaware of our deepest needs and desires. Sometimes we need things and don't know we need them. Sometimes we yearn for things but do not know exactly what we are yearning for. The men and women of every era yearn for connection and relationship with God, because we were made for that. Birds were made to fly, fish were made to swim, and human beings were made to love God and each other.

"Teach us to pray" is the spoken and unspoken desire of every person, in every place and time. It reflects a desire for wisdom, which in turn reflects a desire to learn how to love and discover the best way to live.

## SHARING THE JOY

Weeks after I learned to pray all those years ago, a desire sprang up within me to share with others the incredible joy I was experiencing. When I began speaking and writing, this habit of daily prayer immediately became the core message. I wanted the message to be inspirational, but also practical. I wanted people to see a clear connection between the message I was sharing and how to activate it in their own lives.

For many years, I told my story and encouraged people to commit to a habit of daily prayer. But over time I realized they needed more. They needed to be taught how to pray and they needed a method of prayer. More than twenty years later, still on this quest, I began to ask: What if there was a method of prayer that taught you how to pray as you prayed? That is how I arrived at the Prayer Process.

The Prayer Process is designed to be used by anyone, anywhere, at any time, regardless of their experience in the spiritual life—and it was designed to grow with you.

For thirty years I have been searching for game changers for ordinary people in the spiritual life. Teaching people how to pray is the ultimate game changer, and I would gladly spend the rest of my life doing nothing else. Several years ago, I challenged myself to think about how we could teach millions of people to pray in the way I have described. This is how I developed the Prayer Process. Millions of people have already benefited from this simple approach, which is a testament not only to its simplicity but also to its effectiveness.

The primary reason the Prayer Process is so effective and impactful is because it immediately overcomes many of the obstacles that prevent people from persevering in prayer. It is a method, yes. But it is a method of prayer that actually teaches people to pray as they pray. The first barrier to developing a habit of daily prayer is that most people who feel drawn to pray simply don't know how to do it; they have never been taught. The Prayer Process teaches people to pray.

The Prayer Process requires no mentor, no guide, and no instructions. The process itself is the guide and the instructions. If someone found a card on the street with the Prayer Process printed on it, just by reading the card, he or she would be able to practice this powerful method of prayer. Simply following the seven prompts leads us into a powerful experience of prayer, and at the same time, teaches us how to pray.

The other barrier the Prayer Process breaks down is that it gets people started immediately. You can begin practicing it today. You don't even need to finish reading this book in order to do it and do it well. All you need is an open heart and the 153 words of the Prayer Process. Getting started is half the battle—in fact, it's more than half.

It is also a process that meets us where we are in our spiritual journey. Whether we are advanced or beginner level, the Prayer Process meets us there and leads us gently, step-by-step, to become all God created us to be. If on a particular day we are feeling dry and discouraged, it meets us where we are and leads us to a more hopeful place. If we are feeling elated and encouraged, it meets us there and teaches us to use these gifts for good. It expands or contracts to meet us where we are with what we need. I have often explained that a monk who has spent fifty years dedicated to prayer in a monastery could practice the Prayer Process and have a powerful experience, while someone who has never prayed in his or her life could engage the Prayer Process and have an equally powerful experience.

The Prayer Process is infinitely expandable and contractible. If you went away on a retreat, you could spend hours praying (or journaling) your way through the process, looking not just at the past twenty-four hours, but at the past year—or even your whole lifetime. For example, the first step in the process concerns gratitude. Imagine how long you could speak to God about everything that has ever happened in your life that you are grateful for. On the other hand, perhaps on a particular day you get distracted and don't pray at your regular time, and then the day gets away from you. Rather than going to bed without praying because you don't have the will or the energy to pray for ten minutes, you can shorten the experience. Take just a minute. Yes, one single minute. You can still go through each of the seven steps, but just speak one line to God about one thing in each step. Never let what you can't do interfere with what you can do. This ability to expand and contract is the thing I love the most about the Prayer Process. It is not elitist or exclusionary in any way. It serves all according to how open our hearts are to encountering God.

Finally, the Prayer Process is a form of prayer that teaches us to pray at deeper and deeper levels just by practicing it.

People often ask me, "How do you pray?" This is how I pray. I use the Prayer Process, every day. I lay it before you now as a gift of infinite value and invite you to commit to using it for the next twenty-one days. I am confident that if you do, you will discover it is a game changer for both your inner and outer lives. It is my hope that it will become the context within which you practice your habit of daily prayer for the rest of your life.

## THE PRAYER PROCESS

1.  **Gratitude**: Begin by thanking God in a personal dialogue for whatever you are most grateful for today.

2.  **Awareness**: Revisit the times in the past twenty-four hours when you were and were not the-best-version-of-yourself. Talk to God about these situations and what you learned from them.

3.  **Significant Moments**: Identify something you experienced today and explore what God might be trying to say to you through that event (or person).

4.  **Peace**: Ask God to forgive you for any wrong you have committed (against yourself, another person, or him) and to fill you with a deep and abiding peace.

5.  **Freedom**: Speak with God about how he is inviting you to change your life, so that you can experience the freedom to be the-best-version-of-yourself.

6.  **Others**: Lift up to God anyone you feel called to pray for today, asking God to bless and guide them.

7.  **Finish** by praying the Our Father.

Could 153 words change your life every day, forever? I have seen them change many lives; I hope yours is next.

There are thousands of ways to pray. But we need one method to anchor our habit of prayer. This helps to create a powerful routine, which is essential when establishing a life-giving habit in our lives. If you really want to improve your life and are serious about growing spiritually, this is the method of prayer I recommend to you. Commit yourself to this practice for ten minutes each day and you will advance spiritually like never before.

One of the real treasures the Prayer Process offers is an increased awareness of who we are and what is happening within and around us. This awareness heightens our ability to experience life. That's right, it actually increases our capacity for life. It awakens us from our unconsciousness and invites us to live at the height of consciousness. It also continually increases our awareness of how God is showing up in our lives, how he is at work in the situations and circumstances we face each day.

What percentage of your daily activity are you conscious of? What percentage of your daily activity are you truly present to? You might be surprised.

Think about all the things you do unconsciously every day. You drive to work, taking many turns—are you conscious of each of those turns? Are you conscious of any of them? Or have you become so used to the path that you follow it unconsciously? Often we shave, eat and drink, bathe, and even say "I love you" unconsciously. Very often we wander through a day, a week, a month, or even a year with very little consciousness, almost oblivious to what is really happening inside and around us. The Prayer Process challenges that by liberating us from living unconsciously.

It seems to me that people are becoming less and less aware of themselves. Many of the things we say and do scream: "I am completely unaware of how the way I speak and act affects the people around me!" Prayer heightens our awareness and leads us to experience life on a whole new level—consciously. It awakens us to the miracles that are happening within and around us every day.

Does God speak to us? Yes, and if we listen closely, what I think many of us will hear him saying to us is: "It's time to wake up!"

The Prayer Process provides a consistent format to guide you in your daily prayer. Although it may seem rudimentary, for anyone who has tried to pray and failed, but still yearns to connect with God, it is both a profound and practical gift.

Most people have never been taught how to pray. This is the first barrier they face when moved by the Spirit to pray. The Prayer Process solves this. Just by reading through the process and following the prompts, we learn to pray. The method itself teaches us to pray. The next obstacle most people encounter when they feel drawn to prayer is that they simply don't know where to start. The Prayer Process also solves this by providing a simple format and method.

This method of prayer is a game changer for you spiritually and for every aspect of your life. But don't take my word for it. Commit yourself to practicing the Prayer Process for ten minutes each day for twenty-one days. If you do, I am confident that you will very quickly be convinced of its power. It is 153 words that can change your life forever.

Each of the first six steps in the process should stimulate a conversation between you and God. It is easy to fall into the trap of merely thinking during prayer. When you become aware of yourself doing that, return to actually speaking with God about whatever it is you are thinking. The goal is to develop the ability to have intimate conversations with God during this time set aside for prayer. The more deeply rooted we become in this habit of daily prayer, the more those conversations with God will spill over into the moments of our daily lives—and then we will find ourselves speaking to him as we drive to work, as we wait in line at the market, as we walk the dog, sitting in the waiting room at the doctor's office, and throughout the ordinary activities of our daily lives.

I have been blessed with many wonderful friends in this life. Some of my best friends live down the street and others on the other side of the world; some of my best friends are dead authors, saints, and heroes; I have a handful of books that are among my best friends; and the Prayer Process is one of my best friends. For what is a friend? Anyone (or anything) who wants what is best for you and actively seeks to help you become all God created you to be—the-very-best-version-of-yourself.

The goal of the Prayer Process is to trigger a regular and meaningful conversation between you and God. It also provides the blueprint for creating and sustaining a dynamic habit of daily prayer for the rest of your life. Nothing will change your life more meaningfully than developing a vibrant and sustainable prayer life.

I encourage you to begin (or renew) your commitment to the habit of daily prayer today. Use the Prayer Process to guide you. If you do, I am confident that you will find it is a faithful guide that will lead you deep into a lifelong friendship with God. In this life, there is nothing more important or fulfilling than developing a friendship with God.

Prayer is about relationship, intimacy, and oneness with God. Conversation is at the heart of all dynamic relationships. Talk to God—just talk to him—and before long, you will witness the conversations in all your relationships evolving. Prayer teaches us how to live, and like prayer, life is about relationships.

Just talk to him. . . .

## YOUR BEST DAYS

One of the great moments in the life of a Christian comes when we realize, once and for all, that a life with prayer is better than a life without prayer.

When people are striving to recover from an addiction to drugs or alcohol, they are encouraged not to think about staying clean and sober for the rest of their lives, but to take it one day at a time. If they think about never having another drink, for example, the thought itself can be so overwhelming and seem so impossible that it crushes their spirit and they go back to drinking. If they think about not having a drink today, that seems manageable and possible, and they get one day closer to throwing off the yoke of slavery to alcohol. We establish life-giving habits one day at a time as well. If thinking about praying every day for the rest of your life is overwhelming, just take it one day at a time.

Life is a collection of days, and some days are better than others. This may seem obvious, and so perhaps we don't question it. But why are some days better than others? If you look back over the past couple of months, a few days were probably great, most days were average, some days were not so good, and perhaps there were even a couple of days that were horrible. But what made the difference? Was it something outside your control or something within your influence?

One thing I have discovered as I become more and more conscious of what is happening within and around me is that if a day doesn't get off to a good start, it very rarely finishes as a good day. Once a day gets away from us, we tend to go into survival mode. And a day can get away from us in so many ways. In fact, a day will almost certainly go wrong unless we consciously take the time to focus it first thing each morning.

How do your best days begin? Most people don't know. They have a hunch, but they have simply never thought enough about it or experimented with it. As you begin to practice the habit of daily prayer, and if you begin each day with prayer, I think you will discover this changes the way you enter into and experience your daily life. This knowledge will further empower you to harness prayer to give real direction to your life at the beginning of each day. Begin your day with prayer, however brief. Even if that is not your main time of prayer each day, and even if it is not the time when you use the Prayer Process, begin your day with prayer.

Over time you will become more aware of how praying (or not praying) impacts you, your life, your relationships, your work, your health, your decisions, and every aspect of every day. This growing awareness is ordinary and practical, and yet, it is one of the highest spiritual gifts.

After a while, you will feel the difference when you don't follow your regular prayer routine. You may feel less joyful, unfocused, stressed, less conscious of what is happening inside and around you, less capable of giving those you care about the love and attention they deserve, and disconnected from God. It will be as if you feel disconnected from yourself when you don't start your days in the way that you know works best.

People who have a strong habit of daily prayer know how their best days begin, and the more mature among them (in wisdom, not in age) will do almost anything to defend their morning routine. They would rather get up an hour early than forgo their morning prayer. They know that a day that doesn't start well tends not to end well; it is simply too difficult to shift the momentum of a day.

How do your best days begin? Try beginning your day with prayer, however brief, and observe how it impacts the rest of your day.

## THE BASICS

The mastery of almost anything is about the basics. As human beings, we are fascinated with things that are new and different, special or extraordinary, the latest shiny, sparkly things. But almost all success and happiness in this world is born from ordinary things. We allow ourselves to be seduced by the spectacular, but the basics are where you find the true and lasting treasure.

Success at almost anything rests upon this single principle: Do the basics, do them well, and do them every day, *especially* when you don't feel like doing them. It doesn't matter if it is football, marriage, parenting, personal finances, physical fitness, military operations, small business, big business, or prayer. This is one of the reasons most people don't become phenomenally successful. They lack the persistence to do the same things over and over again.

Mastering the basics is the secret to success. So as we make this journey together, resist the temptation to look beyond the basics. Throwing yourself into the basics day after day may get tedious from time to time, but the peace and joy that come from an established habit of daily prayer never do.

When it comes to establishing a vibrant daily prayer life, the basics are few and simple: what, when, where, how, and why.

**What:** Ten minutes a day in conversational prayer.

**When:** Most people believe it is most impactful to pray in the morning, but some of us are not morning people, and we don't want that to be the reason you don't persevere with this habit. You can decide on the time that sets you up to succeed, but pick a specific time, put it on your schedule, and stick to it. Make it a nonnegotiable part of your day, a sacred commitment. If something comes up and you need to move your prayer time, move it to earlier in the day; never put it off. Once you put it off, it usually does not get done.

**Where:** Find a place where you can be still and quiet, with the fewest possible distractions, a place that is available to you every day. Make any changes you need to make to that space to set yourself up to succeed (though you probably won't know the best way to set up the space until you have prayed there for a while). From time to time, I encourage you to stop by a church for your daily prayer. We read in the Bible about Jesus going to a place set apart to pray. Your church is a place set apart. More specifically, it is designed especially for prayer. This means it is usually quiet. In addition, God is present in a very unique and special way in our churches.

**How:** Using the Prayer Process (and other tools provided in this book). There are thousands of different methods and forms of prayer, but when you are establishing this powerful habit it is best to focus on just one. Develop mastery using this method of prayer before exploring other approaches. The famous martial artist Bruce Lee said, "I am not afraid of the man who has practiced ten thousand kicks once. I am afraid of the man who has practiced one kick ten thousand times." The goal is to deeply ingrain the habit of daily prayer into your soul and life. This goal is best served with the practice of one form of prayer—in this case, the Prayer Process.

**Why:** What people do is interesting, but *why* they do what they do is fascinating. As you enter into greater intimacy with God, he will encourage you to express your reasons and motives for many things you do. This exploration of motive can lead to incredible awareness, as well as to a life lived with laser-focused intentionality. When it comes to prayer, knowing our reasons plays an important role. It allows us to get clear about why we are doing it, which serves as a powerful reminder when we are tempted to skip it, put it off, or stop it altogether. Get crystal clear about your why.

## WHAT IS YOUR IMAGE OF GOD?

Few things will impact our experience of prayer more than the image of God we hold in our hearts. The difficulty is we each have an incomplete and distorted image of God. The Scriptures teach us that we were created in the image of God, but without authentic experiences of God the danger is that we begin to create God in our image. Through the daily habit of prayer and other spiritual practices, our image of God gradually becomes more aligned with the reality of who God is.

What is your image of God? How do you envision God? Do you imagine God as a loving father or as a wrathful father? Do you see Jesus as a teacher, brother, friend, Savior? Do you envision the Holy Spirit as close and personal or distant and impersonal?

The first time I explored these questions I was embarrassed at how little I was able to articulate. I challenged myself to sit down and write everything I knew about God. I was stunned at how little I knew. I challenged myself to make a list of all God's qualities and attributes. I was astonished at how few I could name. This revealed that I didn't know God very well at all.

We assume that we know God. We also assume that what we believe about God is true, and often it is not. The only thing worse than not knowing God, is knowing and believing things about God that aren't true. These are worse than not knowing God at all, because they often prevent us from really getting to know God.

Throughout our lives we have been told things, and had experiences, that have distorted the image of God we hold in our hearts and minds. For example, if your father was neglectful or abusive, that has almost certainly impacted the way you see God. It will particularly affect your ability to see God as a loving and attentive father who is interested in everything that happens in your life. Another example may be things you heard about God at school. You may have been told that God doesn't exist. Some teachers may have made fun of students who believed in God. All these experiences impact the image we hold of God in our hearts and minds. Sometimes we are aware of these influences and sometimes we are not. It may take years or decades to realize how certain people and events have affected our image of God, positively or negatively.

So, what is God really like? God has many attributes. He is infinite, eternal, good, self-sufficient, ever-present, generous, holy, personal, gracious, loving, wise, mysterious, all-powerful, one, providential, righteous, just, transcendent, truthful, eternal, patient, free, immutable, approachable, peaceful, perfect, compassionate, beautiful, praise-worthy, faithful, all-knowing, graceful, merciful, attentive, fascinating and deeply interested in everyone and everything he has created.

There are so many attributes that could be used to describe God,  so it is important to remember what we are trying to accomplish. Our goal is not to gain a theological understanding of God (though we are certainly not opposed to that). Our goal is to discover how you best connect with God.

From time to time, I like to ask myself: What are three attributes that most help you connect with God? These are the three I picked today: loving, patient, and faithful. At other times in my life, I have chosen other attributes.

I chose loving because love seems to be the essence of everything that God is and does, and I yearn for it to be the essence of who I am and all I do. But on a more basic, human level, I yearn to love and be loved. I chose patient because I know my faults, failings, and limitations, and I need him (and anyone I am in relationship with) to be patient with me as I fumble around trying to become a-better-version-of-myself. I chose faithful because I need to remind myself that our God keeps his promises. I find this to be a great reminder and comfort in times of trouble or uncertainty. What are the three attributes that most help you connect with him?

Why does this matter? There are many reasons, but let's begin with three that are intensely practical. The first reason is because the image you hold of God profoundly (or disturbingly) affects the image you hold of yourself. The Scriptures tell us we are made in the image of God, so the way we see ourselves is going to be massively impacted by the way we see God. As a parent I am fascinated with how my children see themselves. The image they hold of themselves holds astounding influence over almost everything they think, say, and do. That doesn't change, no matter how old we become. If our image of God is distorted, the image we hold of ourselves will also be distorted. A healthy image of God will also equip you with an image of yourself that is strong and true.

The second reason it matters, is because your image of God impacts every relationship in your life. We will never have better relationships with other people than our relationship with God. Our relationship with God serves as a model for our other relationships.

The third reason is because nothing will impact your relationship with God more than how you imagine God to be. If you have a distorted image of God, it becomes an obstacle to many of the most significant moments in the spiritual journey.

Through the daily habit of prayer (and other spiritual experiences and practices) our image of God gets adjusted. There is a difference between knowing about someone and actually knowing that person. God is love. This is to know about God. God is loving. This is to experience God in a deeply personal way. Our knowledge about God often outstrips our experience of him, and this book is a direct attempt to tip those scales. Through a daily habit of prayer, we are seeking to experience the loving God who is love. By encountering God regularly, our image of God will continually be realigned with the reality of God.

The image we hold of God impacts everything. Not just our spirituality, but everything. It isn't something we can sit down to discuss for an afternoon and straighten out. There are powerful emotional, psychological, spiritual, and practical influences at work. It takes a lifetime of prayer, reflection, and observation to continually realign our image of God with the reality of who God is.

How well do you know God? I have asked myself this question many times throughout my life, and I keep arriving at the same answer: Better than I did last year, but not as well as I would like to know him.

I know this topic is just a few paragraphs in a book about prayer, but please believe me when I tell you that the implications of your personal image of God are endless. Ask God to reveal himself to you, to re-align how you perceive him with who he really is.

## THERE IS POWER IN A NAME

One of the ways we connect in relationships and conversation is through names. Finding the name that best helps you to connect with God is essential as we learn how to pray.

There is great meaning in names. Parents often agonize over what name to give their child because they know there is power and meaning in a name. God often changed a person's name when he sent him or her on a great mission (Genesis 17:5). In the New Testament we read about demons being cast out in the name of Jesus (Mark 9:38 and Acts 16:18).

Throughout the history of Christianity, it has been believed that the name of Jesus holds power. We could discuss and debate this at length, but I propose a shorter path. Next time you sense danger, temptation, or confusion in your life, repeat the name of Jesus slowly over and over again. "Jesus... Jesus... Jesus..."

The names we use to address each other also signal levels of intimacy. One person may have many names. A man may be known as Mr. Jones, Edward, Ted, and Teddy. My wife knows that if someone calls me Matt they are pretending to know me, but they don't really know me, because nobody close to me calls me Matt. There is power and meaning in names.

Conversation is a path to intimacy and the names we use are signs of intimacy. Finding the name that best helps you to connect with God and enter into conversation with him is essential to establish a vibrant life of prayer. Prayer is after all, among other things, a conversation.

The best place to start is probably Father, Son, and Holy Spirit, if for no other reason than this is how God has revealed himself to us. Over time it is good to learn to pray to each of them and healthy to foster a relationship with each person of the Trinity.

One way to do this is to consider the qualities of God and discern which quality you ascribe to the Father, Son, and Holy Spirit. I have always seen the Holy Spirit as the great encourager, inspiring us and transforming each moment into a mini-Pentecost; Jesus has always been teacher and friend; and, God the Father has always been adviser, guide, and wise counsel.

But it is different for each person, and it is different for you. What's important is that you explore it for yourself and get comfortable with the name that draws you into conversation with God. This daily habit of prayer we are striving to develop is a conversation, a prayer of the heart, and names are intimate and important.

This is not an academic quest, but a deeply personal exploration of which name best helps you to encounter God.

I pray mostly to God the Father. Imagine the most amaz-ing father, all the best of any father you have ever known, with none of the bad. The idea of God as Father resonates with me deeply, and it has always struck me that when the disciples asked Jesus to teach them how to pray, he instruct-ed them to pray to God as Father. But I know people who didn't have great relationships with their earthy fathers who find it very difficult to pray to God as Father. This is not insurmountable, but understandable.

Other people find that praying to Jesus makes it easi-er for them to relate to and encounter God. The Gospels provide so many images and stories of Jesus that stimulate our knowledge and imagination. These are all very help-ful when it comes to praying in the conversational style we have been discussing.

Others relate more easily to God as Spirit and find that praying to the Holy Spirit is the best way for them to en-gage in a deeply personal relationship with God. And I have never met anyone who relied too much on the Holy Spirit for guidance in the moments of the day when we are con-fronted with decisions large and small. In fact, most of us rely too little on the Holy Spirit.

Of course, in different seasons and situations we may find ourselves spontaneously praying to God as Father, Son, or Spirit. And, even within each of the three persons, there are dozens of names by which we may call upon God. Jesus alone is known as Lord, Master, Christ, Logos, Son of God, Son of Man, Son of David, Lamb of God, the New Adam, the Second Adam, the Light of the World, King of the Jews, Rabbi, the King of Kings, the Lord of Lords, the Word made Flesh, Emmanuel, and many others.

Find the name that best facilitates a relationship between you and God. It may take time, but you will be glad you did. Lord, Yahweh, Spirit of God, Adonai, Father, Jesus... find what works for you... and sometimes the way to find what works for you is to pray using different names. As you address God using different names, pay attention to which name resonates most deeply. You will know it when you find it. You may already know it. It may change over time, and that's okay. Our relationship with God should be by its very nature dynamic: positive, full of life and energy, changing and growing, a force that stimulates change and progress.

The name (or names) we use to address God is important, and yet, just the beginning of the intimacy God desires to have with you. The tenderness of God is such that he has care and concern for each and every single one of his children. His providence is another expression of his tenderness. This tenderness is also one of God's attributes that we don't speak of enough.

Talking to God is a beautiful and intimate act. Calling out to God by name was considered so intimate by many religions throughout history that they have not dared to do it. Christianity is very different in this respect. We believe in a personal God, who is close to us and has concern for our well-being, not in a cold, distant, and unapproachable deity. The idea of choosing the name which most helps you connect intimately with God would seem blasphemous to many religions past and present, and yet, it is very natural and normal for a Christian to foster his or her intimate relationship with God in this simple and profound way.

## BEGIN TODAY

The hardest part of many things is getting started. A space shuttle uses 96 percent of its fuel during takeoff, but once it is launched, it continues on with little effort relative to what is required to get it into the atmosphere. The first twenty-one days of a new habit are like the launch of a space shuttle. Don't miss a single day. Guard diligently against resistance, laziness, and distractions.

Have you begun your habit of daily prayer yet? If not, what are you waiting for? Don't wait to finish the book. Don't wait another day. Begin today! If you have to choose between praying and reading the next chapter of this book, pray—pray, I beg you. The sooner you begin the habit, the deeper the habit will take root in your life. And your life will be forever changed and renewed because of it.

God is constantly inviting us to grow, to develop, to

change, to love more deeply, and to become the whole person he created us to be. This requires a daily conversion of the heart. Begin each day in prayer. Make this a sacred appointment on your calendar. Do not set your course for the day alone—seek the wise counsel of your captain. He will help you to avoid dangerous waters and rocks. And begin each time of prayer by renewing your availability to God.

Never miss your daily prayer time. If something comes up, move it forward; never put your prayer off. If you do, you will almost inevitably find yourself at the end of the day having been busy with so many things that mean so little in the grand scheme of things, but not having spent time with God in this powerful and personal way. Make a promise to yourself and to the one who gave you the very breath that animates your being. If we cannot set aside these few minutes to spend exclusively with God each day, we will not make ourselves available to him throughout the day. If we do not make ourselves available to him entirely for the promised time, it will be too easy to exclude him from the other parts of our days and lives. Make a promise and keep that promise, one day at a time.

I often wonder why my writings resonate with so many people. One of the reasons I have settled upon over the years is because I am an observer—of self, others, and life.

My wife, Meggie, and I have been blessed with five beautiful children. It is one of the great joys of my life to spend time with them, but I have also learned many lessons by simply observing them. One of the most practical gifts my wife has given our children since they were born has been routine. It seems so ordinary, yet it is often the ordinary things that are most essential and most life-giving. Children thrive on routine. I have witnessed it. Take the routine away and chaos reigns. They will resist the routine, complain about it, wrestle with it, but they need it, and it brings out the best in them.

Adults thrive on routine too. Let this, your habit of daily prayer, be the beginning of many powerful new routines in your life, so you may flourish like never before.

## SOUL NOTE:

*Soul,*
*Come to the silence and learn what it is that you need to thrive.*
*Embrace what it is that makes you dance for joy.*
*And share with everyone you meet*
*the love that Love himself has filled you with.*

# PART FOUR

## Six Powerful Spiritual Lessons

FOR THOUSANDS OF YEARS, men and women of all faiths have been making pilgrimages. These sacred journeys are powerful experiences that people make in search of God, his will, and his favor. Most of all, these sacred journeys remind us that life itself is a pilgrimage, and that we are just passing through this place we call earth.

Many of these pilgrimages involve hundreds and even thousands of miles of travel, and before modern transportation they were grueling undertakings. But contrary to popular belief, the longest and most difficult pilgrimage in the world has never been to Jerusalem or Santiago or Fatima.

## THE LONGEST JOURNEY

The Sioux believed that the longest journey we can make in this life is from the head to the heart. This is also the longest spiritual journey we can make; it is the pilgrimage of prayer. We think of the heart as emotional, and it is, but it is also deeply spiritual. Are you living your life from the mind? Are you living your life from the heart? Or have you found the delicate balance between the heart and the mind that allows you to live in growing wisdom? Prayer helps us make the journey from the head to the heart, and it is prayer that allows us to balance the heart and mind so that we can live in wisdom.

Every journey has a series of ordinary moments, but there are other moments that stand out as significant. The significant moments on the pilgrimage of our lives usually present us with a choice that needs to be made. There is a great spiritual decision before you right now: To make prayer a daily habit in your life or not? This is a choice that will affect you every day for the rest of your life.

Will you choose to make this journey by adopting a habit of daily prayer? If you do, there are six key moments that you will encounter on your journey. I have encountered them, and I want to prepare you for them by making you aware of them. Each of these moments represents an enormous shift in the inner life. They are critical points in the journey that provide enduring lessons that will serve us well for the rest of our lives.

You will never be the same after experiencing these moments. They are truly seismic. Even if you abandon the way of prayer after experiencing them, they will live in you forever as an insatiable longing for something more, better, and beautiful. Pray you have the grace, wisdom, and courage to embrace them when you encounter these moments.

## SIX SEISMIC SHIFTS

Over the past thirty years, I have experienced many seasons in my spiritual life: long stretches of great consistency; other stretches when I have been inconsistent in my prayer; times of resistance and times of surrender; seasons of great patience and seasons of selfish impatience; periods when I couldn't wait to get to prayer and periods when I had to force myself to keep showing up; days when I felt the warmth of God's love fill my whole being and days when I felt so cold it seemed he could not be further away from me; weeks when I felt I was in the thickest fog and months when I saw things with great clarity; seasons of trial when nothing seemed to go right and seasons of triumph when it seemed nothing could go wrong.

The spiritual life is made up of seasons, and even in the darkest moments it is important to remind ourselves that spring will come again.

The six lessons I am about to share with you have served me well in every season.

The definition of seismic is "of enormous proportions or effect"; I use that word very deliberately here. The six lessons I am about to describe to you had that kind of impact on my inner and outer life, and I am confident they will also have great impact on your life.

## THE FIRST SHIFT:
## BEGIN THE CONVERSATION

The first of these seismic shifts is wonderfully ordinary and beautifully simple. Imagine you are walking through Central Park in New York City and you stop at one of the many benches to rest a little. On the next bench sits an elderly man. After catching your breath and taking in the scene, you say hello to him. From there a delightful conversation starts up, and before you know it you have been talking for who knows how long. The surprise and delight create a buoyant feeling within you, yet it is more than just a feeling. You get up to leave and carry on with your other commitments for the day, but you feel compelled to ask the elderly gentleman if you can stay in touch. He agrees and gives you his contact information. It is the beginning of a unique friendship. You know it right then and there. It is yours to treasure or to squander.

Prayer is a conversation. Just begin the conversation. This is the first seismic shift in the spiritual life. Once the conversation has begun, it can lead anywhere. Most important, it will lead to the places it needs to lead to. Never underestimate how important it is to just begin the conversation. This is true with your friends and colleagues, your brothers and sisters, children and spouse, and of course with God. Strike up a conversation and you will be amazed where he leads you.

This first shift requires us to make the journey from the head to the heart, to turn from a thinking type of prayer to a relational style of prayer. It is simple, but not easy. The Prayer Process is designed to facilitate this conversation between you and God, so you can learn to pray with your heart, and make the journey from head to heart.

Just start the conversation. This was the first of the six seismic shifts in my inner life. I had no idea that day when I stepped into that church with my friend that I was about to begin the most epic conversation of my life.

## THE SECOND SHIFT:
## ASK GOD WHAT HE WANTS

The second of these seismic shifts occurs within the conversation when we stop asking God for what we want and start asking what he wants.

The majority of prayers mumbled and muttered, whispered and screamed on the planet today will be asking God for something. We ask for special favors, everything from the honorable to the frivolous. We ask him to help our sick friend get better, to find us a job, to help our addicted relative, to help us make it to work on time.

I remember standing on a soccer field praying that God would help us win. Knowing what I know today about life, all the human suffering and the very real unmet needs of so many people, if I were back on that soccer field today I wouldn't be praying that prayer.

This shift in our spiritual lives when we stop asking God for what we want and start asking what he wants is seismic because this is when we begin to ask the Big Question: "God, what do you think I should do?" "God, what do you think I should do in this situation. . . at home, work, with my friend, with my son, with my mother?" "God, what do you think I should focus on in my relationship with my children?" "God, what area of my marriage should I work on growing?" And ultimately, "God, what do think I should do with the rest of my life?"

When we start asking God for advice, direction, inspiration, and guidance, this is a significant moment. It marks a real shift in our spirituality. When we stop asking him for things, for favors, and for our will to be done, we begin to open ourselves to much more than his will. We open ourselves to his wisdom. As we mature spiritually, we realize that to want anything other than the will of God is foolish and futile. But in the early stages of our spiritual development, the will of God can seem heavy, restrictive, burdensome, even though the opposite is true.

The other thing that happens when we ask God about his ways and plans is we begin to adopt a spiritual curiosity. This curiosity about God and his dreams for us and the world can be incredibly invigorating. It transforms the way we see ourselves, other people, creation, society, and indeed God.

This doesn't mean that we never ask God for anything—it is natural and normal for a child to ask his or her loving father for something—it just means that the focus of our prayer changes. There is a time and a place to ask God for things, but just as it would be inappropriate to be constantly asking someone for something in a relationship, it shouldn't be the focus of our prayer.

## THE THIRD SHIFT:
## GIVE YOURSELF TO PRAYER

The third seismic shift that occurs in the inner life is when we stop *doing* our prayer and start giving ourselves to prayer.

Giving yourself to prayer means showing up and letting God do what he wants to do with you during that time of prayer. It means letting go of expectations and agendas for our time with God. It means detachment from the feelings that prayer provokes within us.

In *The Seven Levels of Intimacy*, I introduced the concept of carefree timelessness. Carefree timelessness is the reason young people fall in love so easily, and the lack of carefree timelessness is the reason so many couples forget their story together and fall out of love. What is carefree timelessness? Time together without an agenda. Married couples with young children have very little carefree timelessness, and probably none unless they set out to intentionally create it.

The third seismic shift of the spiritual life is about moving prayer from something we do to something we give ourselves to. This shift requires us to surrender to the experience and to believe that God is working in us even when it feels like we are not accomplishing anything. It is about enjoying some carefree timelessness with God.

What makes it difficult is that so much of our lives is focused on doing and accomplishing. This requires us to let go and focus on being. But once again prayer is teaching us how to live, because the problem many of us have in our relationships of every type is the inability to let go and just be.

The shift from doing prayer to giving ourselves to prayer may seem subtle, but the reality is, this is one of the most significant inner changes that can take place in our souls.

# THE FOURTH SHIFT:
# TRANSFORM EVERYTHING INTO PRAYER

The daily habit of prayer leads us to recognize God presence in every aspect and moment of our lives. Not that he is in our presence, but that we are continually in his presence. Prayer is not an activity that encompasses a small portion of our days. It is a way of life. To pray is to live in the presence of God. As we commit ourselves to a daily practice of prayer, our spiritual senses begin to awaken, and we become aware of God at our side throughout the day.

The stronger our connection with God, the more easily we recognize his presence in every moment of every day. There are moments in life that are so arresting that even the most spiritually unaware person cannot help but recognize God's presence. The first time a newborn baby smiles, most people are stricken with an awe and a recognition that God is present. It is much harder to recognize God in the pain of a beggar on the street or in the eyes of someone you do not particularly like.

In each moment, "God is with us (Matthew 1:23)." This is not just the message of Christmas, but the message of every day: God is with us, in each moment. Every moment is a precious gift, and the present moment is where God resides. It is the only place he can be found. Jesus said, "Remember, I am with you always (Matthew 28: 20). Always, not sometimes. He didn't want us looking for him in the past or the future. God is not around the corner or over the next hill; he is by our side.

God is with us when we wash the dishes, when we change the baby's diaper, when we mow the lawn, when we make love to our spouse, commute to work, have dinner with our family, take care of a sick relative, pay the bills and work on our budget, talk to our children, and when we hold hands with a friend. Always, everywhere, and in everything, God is with us.

That's why everything is prayer.

Washing the dishes is prayer.

Changing the baby's diaper is prayer.

Mowing the lawn is prayer.

Commuting to work is prayer.

Having dinner with your family is prayer.

Taking care of a sick relative is prayer.

Paying the bills and working on your budget is prayer.

Talking to your children is prayer.

Holding hands and making love with your spouse is prayer.

The fourth seismic shift occurs when we discover that every activity can be transformed into prayer by offering it to God.

"Pray constantly" was St. Paul's invitation, and it is a beautiful principle of the spiritual life. But if most people have not been taught how to pray and establish a habit of daily prayer in their lives, you can be certain they have not been taught how to transform the ordinary moments of their days into prayer.

Every honest human activity can be transformed into prayer.

Learning to transform daily activities into prayer was one of the greatest spiritual lessons of my life. And it is so simple. Offer the next hour of your work for a friend who is sick. Offer the task you are least looking forward to today to God as a prayer for the person you know who is suffering most today, and do that task with great love, better than you have ever done it. Offer each task, one at a time, to God as a prayer for a specific intention, and do so with love. Pray for others as they come to mind throughout the day.

This is how we are able to keep the epic conversation going, this never-ending conversation between you and God—by acknowledging him in the activities and affairs of our lives. Prayer is the conversation of a lifetime, and a lifetime of conversation. It's ongoing and constant. And what is more important than this conversation?

If you were having lunch with God, would you leave to attend to some other matter? If you were on the phone with God, who or what would be important enough that you would put him on hold? Everything is trivial compared to God, and even the most mundane task becomes abundantly meaningful when we include God.

As you go off into the busy happenings of your day, God is saying, "Take me with you! Let me come along and keep you company." By recognizing him at our side in each moment, we include him in everything we do. And when we include him, the mere knowledge of his presence leads us to seek out behaviors, people, and experiences that are good for us and avoid those that are not.

Guide God around your life.

"Lord, we are going to have lunch with my friend Anthony today. He has had a hard time in his marriage lately; please encourage him."

"Lord, this is going to be a difficult meeting. I believe the best outcome for everyone involved is if we agree to partner on this project, but I think their lead negotiator wants to part ways so he can get a bigger piece of the deal for himself. Please open the hearts and minds of everyone at the table to what is really going on here."

"Lord, It's been a tough day, stressful in many ways, and I am just worn out. Please help me to enter my home with patience and calm, and to love my wife and children as if it were the last time I were ever going to see them."

In this way, your whole life becomes a prayer, an epic conversation with God. This constant litany of prayers for the people in your life, calling God's grace and mercy upon all who cross your path is truly an elevated way of living.

The more we engage in this epic conversation the more powerful our connection with God becomes, and the more we become his ambassadors of peace and love in the world. As time passes, people begin to notice there is something different about your presence. It is palpable. Then merely by meeting someone for lunch or coffee, we are ushering them into the presence of God, sharing his peace, joy, love, and wisdom with them. In this way, we begin to embody the prayer of Saint Francis: "Lord, make me an instrument of your peace."

The daily habit of prayer raises our consciousness to recognize God present and at work in our lives. The time we set aside each day for prayer brings clarity to our lives and our choices. It liberates us from the expectations that get placed upon us by other people and the world in general. It also liberates us from the expectations we place on ourselves.

This daily habit of prayer teaches us to recognize God's presence throughout the day and transform each part of our day into prayer. This is a beautiful way to live. Is there beauty in the way you are living your life? This is a simple way to infuse your life with beauty. Begin today.

## THE FIFTH SHIFT:
## MAKE YOURSELF AVAILABLE

Do you wish to know the secret to supreme happiness? Strip away everything in your heart and set aside all in your life that makes you less available to God. The joy we experience is proportional to how available we make ourselves to God.

The fifth shift is about making ourselves 100 percent available to God.

Many years ago, I walked the Camino, the old road to Santiago de Compostela. In preparing, I had studied the route and researched what to take with me. The guidebooks were emphatic that you should not take more than twenty pounds of provisions in your backpack. At first, I thought this impossible. How was I to survive for almost a month with so little? I stuffed that backpack till it was brimming with stuff.

At the end of the first day, I left a couple of things behind in the hostel for another pilgrim who might need them. The same happened over the next several days until, by day six, I had reduced what I'd thought I would need to what I actually needed. But as the journey went on, I found I needed less and less. By the time I arrived in Santiago, my backpack was slack and more than half-empty.

We need so little. We need so much less than we think we do. This was one of the great lessons of that pilgrimage, and unfortunately a lesson I have had to learn many times before and since. We need so little, but we burden ourselves with so much. And every unnecessary thing we burden ourselves with creates an obstacle between us and God. Every little thing, however small and inconsequential, makes us less available to God. It is also a lesson that you don't need to travel to the other side of the world to learn.

When I returned home, I started systematically unburdening myself of things. I sent items to charities that serve the poor, I gave things away to people who needed them more than I did, neighbors came by to borrow something and I told them to keep it because I didn't need it anymore. The more that was gone, the better I felt. I felt lighter and freer.

Time passed and I went back into hunting-and-gathering mode. Things began to accumulate once again. I slipped into that unconscious mode of living, that state in which we don't do things intentionally, but the momentum of the culture and the gravity of life just take over. Before I knew it, I had more unnecessary stuff than ever before. The difference was this time I had constructed elaborate justifications for why I had to have these things. But it was obvious I was deceiving myself, and so another purge would begin.

I would like to say I have learned this lesson once and for all, but we often need to learn lessons more than once. In the spiritual journey we often take old familiar detours. We fill our lives with stuff—material possessions, social commitments, a disproportionate attachment to our work, an obsessive hobby . . . it could be so many things. You know what they are for you, and I know what they are for me, and they rent space in our minds. They cloud our heart and our judgment, which prevents us from making great decisions. They create obstacles between us and God. They keep us from making ourselves available to God, and therefore prevent us from experiencing the ecstasy of emptying ourselves and allowing God to fill us up.

Empty yourself so that God can fill you up. You will never be sorry that you did. I have experienced the emptiness of selfishness, and I have experienced the ecstasy of emptying myself so that God could fill me. The first is like drinking salt-water to quench your thirst; the second is like drinking deeply from the purest water you have ever tasted. For the first time in my life, I felt truly satisfied. I yearn for you to experience that same satisfaction.

Strip away everything that makes you less available to God. This process of stripping everything else away is one of the defining experiences as we enter deeply into the inner life. Prayer is ultimately about making ourselves available to God. So is life.

Through prayer our spiritual awareness is constantly fine-tuned, and the more fine-tuned it becomes, the more we come to see that so few things really matter. The challenge, then, is to focus on the things that really matter. Is your life focused on the things that matter most? I am ashamed to say that too often I ask myself this question and the answer is no.

Make space for God in your life. This is an essential part of this great spiritual journey we are embarking on. We crowd God out of our lives by filling our lives with things that don't matter. Remove the things that don't matter to make space for God in your life—in your heart, mind, and soul. He will occupy whatever space you make available to him. Whatever space you make available to God, he will fill with unimaginably good things.

Strip away everything that makes you less available to God, make yourself more available to him today than yesterday, and before too long, you will arrive at the fifth seismic shift. At the core of this seismic shift in our spirituality is making ourselves available to God.

The fifth seismic shift in the spiritual life is availability. It is about surrendering ourselves, our plan, and our lives to God. It is through this surrender that our ultimate transformation takes place. It is through this surrender that we make ourselves 100 percent available to God, allowing him to transform us and our lives into everything he imagined for us from the beginning of time.

How available are you to God? Are you ready to surrender and make yourself completely available to him?

You will know when you are ready, and as soon as you are, my advice is: Don't delay. Do not say you'll do it tomorrow. Do not say you're not ready. But I suspect just reading this book and pondering these ideas has prepared your heart, mind, and soul.

God always transforms men and women to the extent that we make ourselves available to him. For many years, I have been encouraging people to make themselves available to God, surrender to him, and allow him to transform them and their lives.

This is a prayer I wrote to help people embrace the initial moment of surrender. It is one I pray often, because I find it helps me to renew that surrender.

Let us pray it together:

*Lord,*
*Here I am.*
*I trust that you have an incredible plan for me.*
*Today I surrender my whole being to your care.*
*I surrender my life, my plans, and my very self to you.*
*I make myself 100 percent available to you today.*
*Transform me. Transform my life.*
*Everything is on the table.*
*Take what you want to take,*
*and give what you want to give.*
*Transform me into the person you created me to be,*
*so I can live the life you envisioned for me at the beginning of time.*
*I hold nothing back.*
*I am 100 percent available.*
*Lead me, challenge me, encourage me,*
*and open my eyes to all your amazing possibilities.*
*Show me what it is you want me to do, and I will do it.*
*Amen.*

The secret to supreme happiness is to strip away everything in your heart and set aside everything in your life that makes you less available to God, and then surrender yourself to his loving plans and care.

## THE SIXTH SHIFT:
## JUST KEEP SHOWING UP!

The most practical wisdom I have ever received about prayer was from an old priest many years ago, when I was first starting to take my spiritual journey seriously. The initial excitement had worn off and I was experiencing the early signs of dryness and desolation in prayer. Our natural and very human reaction is to wonder what we are doing wrong when prayer doesn't "feel good." We often aren't doing anything wrong, and prayer should never be judged by how it makes us feel. Prayer isn't about feelings.

"Just keep showing up," the old priest said to me. When I asked him what he meant, he replied, "I'm speaking plainly. No hidden meanings, boy. Just keep showing up. Show up each day regardless of how you feel or if it is convenient. Just show up and let God work on you."

This is the sixth seismic shift. It occurs when showing up for our daily prayer is no longer a daily decision. It becomes a commitment, a decision that no matter what I am going to show up and be with God for that time each day.

The only failure in prayer is to stop praying. You will think and feel things, and many of them don't mean what you initially think they mean. So keep showing up and sit with whatever it is that God says to you and reveals to you. Over time you will see that some things stay and others pass away. And that's OK. Just keep showing up.

Some days prayer will seem easy and others it will seem difficult. How it seems is never a good indication of how fruitful prayer is. Try not to judge your prayer. It is foolish to say, "I prayed well today." It takes at least ten years to determine whether you prayed well today. Just keep showing up.

If God gives you the grace of encouragement and inspiration, fabulous. Accept it, embrace it, put it to good use, and don't squander it. But if you come away from prayer discouraged on some days, remember that Jesus died on the cross and that was an immense victory. Still, don't see that as an invitation to a life of misery that you design for yourself by creating crosses that God never intended you to carry. Life will bring you enough suffering and challenges without you looking for more. Again, just keep showing up and God will teach you all these things and so many others.

For myself, though there have been times when prayer has seemed effortless, for the most part it doesn't come particularly easily. There are days when I have more enthusiasm for it than other days. And there are days when it is difficult. It requires me to force myself to do it. And of course, there are days when it's wonderful and blissful. It all just depends on what God is doing.

Along the way there will be long and dusty roads, epic mountaintop experiences, moments of fear and trembling in the dark valleys, beautiful mornings filled with hope, and long dark nights that smell like hopelessness. Throughout our journey we will need an ever-flowing stream of practical insights to help us take the next step, but none will serve us better than the simple wisdom of that old priest, "Just keep showing up!"

No matter what, just keep showing up. I find it helps if we remember, it is not about what we are doing. It's about what God is doing in us, through us, and with us—when we show up.

## SIX LIFE-CHANGING AWAKENINGS

It is important to remember that God does all the heavy lifting in the spiritual life. These are things that God does in us. All he asks us to do is open ourselves to him and co-operate. If we start feeling overwhelmed spiritually, there is a fairly good chance that we have confused our role with God's role.

These six significant moments are markers along the way in your sacred journey. But your journey will be as unique and different as a sunset. No two are the same. There are things about them that make them all beautiful and similar, and still they are astoundingly unique.

There will be other significant lessons, shifts, moments in your journey. These are not the only six. But they are six that we all experience when we take the journey of the soul seriously.

**First**: Begin the Conversation
**Second**: Ask God What He Wants
**Third**: Give Yourself to Prayer
**Fourth**: Transform Everything into Prayer
**Fifth**: Make Yourself Available
**Sixth**: Just Keep Showing Up!

There are no rules that say you have to be a certain age before you can embrace these great spiritual lessons. There are no worldly conditions or requirements. There is nothing preventing you from beginning to practice each of these epic spiritual lessons today. You don't need an advanced degree in theology, philosophy, or spirituality to embrace them. All you need to do is respond to the desire that the Holy Spirit is stirring in your soul right now.

Along the way, be mindful that the spiritual life is not a straight line. It is not a checklist of items to work through. Everyone does not encounter them in the same order. There will be steps forward and steps back. Learn from the steps back. It is also easy to regress from talking to God in prayer to just thinking about stuff. It is part of the journey. It is easy to slip back from asking God what he wants to telling him what you want. It is part of the journey. It is easy to revert from giving ourselves to prayer to mechanically doing our prayer. And there will be days when you take back all you have surrendered to God. It is all part of the journey.

In the spiritual life, ground that is won today can be easily lost tomorrow. For this reason, it is essential that we guard our hearts and remain ever vigilant of the people and things that seek to steal us away from what matters most. How? Place the daily habit of prayer at the center of your life. Make it a non-negotiable sacred daily commitment.

---

## SOUL NOTE:

*Soul,*
*As you stumble and fumble toward ecstasy,*
*learn to listen to the voice of the one who created you.*
*He speaks gently to you throughout the day,*
*and delights in those moments when you sit with him in*
*solitude.*

---

# PART FIVE

# The God Who Gave Us Laughter

**THERE ARE SO MANY** opportunities each day to catch a glimpse of the genius of God. One of my favorites is laughter. The genius behind humor and laughter is God. Laughter is essential to the human experience, and humor has been observed in every culture, in every place and time. Can you imagine life without laughter?

## DOES GOD HAVE A SENSE OF HUMOR?

The genius of God is evident in laughter. Laughter is medicine for the body, mind, and soul. Its benefits are endless.

Modern medicine has discovered that laughter strengthens your immune system, improves mood, and diminishes pain. Laughter is a powerful form of stress relief. It burns calories, eases anxiety, reduces stress, and is a natural antidepressant. A good laugh relaxes the body, eases tension, and leaves your muscles relaxed for up to forty-five minutes. Laughter stimulates your heart and increases the number of endorphins released by your brain, which creates an overall sense of well-being. When you laugh, the amount of oxygen-rich air that rushes to your lungs increases. Laughter reduces blood pressure, increases blood flow, and can help protect you from a heart attack. It increases happiness, reduces anger and other negative emotions, and increases resilience in the face of obstacles and unpleasant events. Laughter increases our energy and enthusiasm for life. People who laugh regularly are more joyful and have healthier hearts. Humor improves personal satisfaction, strengthens relationships, helps defuse conflict, shifts our perspective, and attracts other people to us. Laughter connects us with others, makes our burdens seem lighter, and can reduce anger and conflict. It creates a sense of belonging and bonds people together. It enhances teamwork and improves productivity. Laughter and humor build trust, encourage collaboration, increase likability, draw people in to listen, improve memory and retention, make arguments more persuasive, and increase learning by reducing classroom anxiety. Laughter releases serotonin, which improves

focus, decision making, problem solving, objectivity, open-
ness to new ideas, and overall brainpower.

It took some really smart scientists to discover all this,
but God is the genius who is alive and well in laughter.

All this may leave us wondering: Does God have a sense
of humor?

Humor is essential to the human experience. Many of
the most memorable and meaningful moments in life are
humorous. But where is humor in our experience of God,
religion, and spirituality?

If you read the life and teachings of Jesus as portrayed
in the four Gospels, there is little evidence to suggest that
he had a sense of humor. Do you believe that Jesus *didn't*
have a sense of humor? I believe he had a wonderful sense
of humor. I imagine him walking down the dusty roads of
Galilee with his disciples. Thirteen guys spending all that
time together. There must have been some epic moments
of humor. Wouldn't you love to hear Jesus laugh? Wouldn't
you love to know what made him laugh and how he made
others laugh?

For some reason, nobody thought it was important
enough to record, and we have been making the same mis-
take by excluding humor and laughter from our relationship with God ever since. Just as humor is essential to the
human experience, maybe it is also essential to our spiritual
experience.

There is an old joke about making God laugh. It is often

repeated and rarely questioned, but we will question it together now. "If you want to hear God laugh," the joke goes, "tell him your plans." If you think about it, this theory is tragically flawed. What kind of father would laugh at his children when they tell him their plans? In the joke God is laughing at us—or is he laughing at our plans, or our innocence, or our ignorance, or our arrogance? What kind of God would laugh at his children in any of these ways? Not the God I believe in.

I am a father, broken and imperfect, but I cannot imagine laughing at my children's plans. The Scriptures tell us that God delights in his children. And God has taught me to delight in listening to what is going on inside my children's hearts and minds. When they honor me by sharing their hopes and thoughts, I am fascinated. How much more does God, in his infinite goodness, delight when we open our hearts and minds to him?

So, it is impossible for me to conjure an image of a God who laughs at his children or their plans, however misguided they may be at times. But it is equally impossible for me to subscribe to an image of a God with no sense of humor. Does the God who gave us laughter not laugh himself? Does the God who gave us laughter have no sense of humor?

I yearn to know more and more the God who gave us laughter.

# I HEARD GOD LAUGH

The more we get to know God, the more we desire to know him. After I was first taught to pray, I developed an insatiable desire to spend time in prayer.

In the latter half of my teens, my life changed unexpectedly, radically, and forever. It is clear to me now that if I had not been taught how to pray, none of what then unfolded would have been possible. In a sense, on that day when John taught me how to pray, tens of millions of lives were being touched. All the people who would ever read my books or come to hear me speak were the beneficiaries of his bold and brave choice that day.

Never underestimate how impactful some of the small things God calls you to do may end up being.

Being taught to pray was a singular grace beyond all measure, which is why I have always been so passionate about sharing that gift in my own imperfect way with as many people as possible.

As I shared earlier in the book, I began by spending ten minutes each day in prayer. It changed my life. And it filled me with a desire to pray more. I would stop by my church and sit toward the back, and there was something about that time with God that filled me with peace. Before long ten minutes became thirty minutes, and then an hour. I was hungry to grow spiritually. Eventually, I began to experience a timelessness in prayer. I would sit there in that empty church for hours—three, four, five at a time. The priest got sick of waiting for me to leave so he could lock up the church, so he gave me a key and told me to lock up when I was done. "Where have you been?" my mother would ask when I arrived home late for dinner, having lost all track of time.

For almost three years, all I did was go to school, work, play sports, and pray. I spent thousands of hours in that church and other churches around Sydney in those three years. It was during that time in my life that God schooled me in silence and stillness. That was one of the happiest times of my life. I didn't know it at the time, but it was an apprenticeship. God was preparing me for mission, but how could I have known?

I don't speak about this very often, because I would not like anyone to read this and think thousands of hours of prayer are required. That is how God chose to prepare me for what he was calling me to. He may be able to accomplish more with you in ten minutes than he could with me in three hours. And what I am certain of is that he will lead you to whatever experience of prayer you need to fulfill his mission for you. At the same time, I think it would be disingenuous not to share that this was part of the journey that led me to the ministry God was calling me to.

"Be still and know that I am God," the Scriptures counsel us (Psalm 46:10). I believe it. Be still and quiet for long enough and God will reveal himself to you in ways you never dreamed. Learn to be still, learn to be quiet, and God will touch you in profound ways. Sit with God for long enough and amazing things will happen.

In those timeless hours of stillness and silence with God, I experienced so many wonderful things. It was there, deep in the silence, that I first heard God laugh.

I remember the moment. It's not the kind of thing you forget. It was early evening and I was sitting alone in the church of my childhood. It was a Tuesday. I had stopped in on the way home from college and had been sitting there for hours, though I didn't realize it at the time. Back then, time seemed to stand still when I stepped into that old church. There was a carefree timelessness to it all.

Until now I have never mentioned this to a soul, because of all the questions you probably have in your mind right now. What was it like? What did it sound like? What do you mean when you say you heard God laugh? Did you hear it in your heart or mind, or did you hear a clear and audible laugh out loud?

What does God's laughter sound like? It sounds like the smile of a newborn baby; it sounds like a bird flying high in the sky; it sounds like the anticipation of a first kiss; it sounds like a new beginning, a fresh start, the morning breeze; it sounds like the love of the most amazing father you could ever imagine; it sounds like a long drink of cold water after a day in the scorching sun; it sounds like the beach and the mountains; it sounds like the roar of a lion, and the gentle touch of a mother as her child rests. When God laughs, all your senses become one and your whole being radiates joy from the depths of your soul.

It is impossible to describe, and like you and I, God has many laughs, one perfectly suited for each situation. But we can be sure that the God who created us to have a marvelous sense of humor also has a marvelous sense of humor and loves to laugh.

How does hearing God laugh change you? It brings startling clarity to your life about what matters and what doesn't. It fills you with a desire to love God more than anything on this earth, and to accomplish that by loving people more than they love themselves.

The reason I have kept it to myself all these years is because I feared these questions, and I knew that each question would chip away at the experience, diminishing it in some way. I am telling you about it now because I very much want you to have your own experience. I cannot promise you will hear God laugh, because there is nothing any of us can do to make it happen. But I can lead you to where it happens. I can show you how to wait patiently and ready yourself to encounter God in new and wonderful ways. Not because I am different or special, but because for some reason all those years ago, he decided to lead me to that place himself.

I often wonder where I would be today if someone had not taught me how to pray. It sends a shudder up my spine when I think about it. It scares me. I look back on those days when I was a teenager, spending all those hours with God in church. It was an amazing time in my life. Today, I cannot spend that kind of time in prayer. More to the point, I am not called to spend that much time in prayer, and you may never be called to do so. That's why I have spoken so rarely of it over the past thirty years. It was a season in my life, a season with a reason. Maybe I will have another season like that later in my life. I don't know, though I do yearn for it.

Being willing to go to the deep places is not about the amount of time we spend set apart from daily activity in prayer. Going to the deep places with God is about trusting him, making ourselves available to him, committing to a habit of daily prayer, and being mindful of his presence in each moment throughout the day. He wants to laugh with you and cry with you, listen to you and speak to you.

Ask God to draw you deeper into the mysteries of the spiritual life. It is a request he will not refuse, and the wonders he will reveal to you will leave you awestruck—and change your life forever.

## THE DEEP WATERS

The world will serve you an endless supply of shallow and superficial options for every aspect of your life, but none of these will satisfy your soul. The culture prefers to keep people unthinking, unconscious, unaware, and unavailable to God, because people in this state are easily manipulated.

The spiritual life is a constant invitation to go beyond the shallow and superficial offerings of this world and seek out the deep places. It is in these deep waters that the most wonderful spiritual experiences await us all.

There are some fabulous moments in the life of Jesus when he directs people to do things that seem counterintuitive. One of my favorites is when he instructs some of the disciples to let down their nets in the deep water, promising a great catch. Peter points out, "We have worked hard all night and haven't caught anything" (Luke 5:4–5).

When we are reading the Scriptures, it is important that we don't skip over the beautiful moments of humanity. Peter and his friends were professional fishermen. They had been out fishing all night. They had "worked hard." So he is essentially saying to Jesus, "If there were fish, we would have caught some." But what Jesus was saying had nothing to do with fish or fishing. He was really asking, "Do you trust me?" They did. So they let down their nets in the deep water and caught so many fish that their nets began to break, their boats began to sink from the weight of the catch, and they had to call upon their friends on boats nearby to help them haul in the massive number of fish.

God introduces an element into every situation that is both predictable and unpredictable. It is predictable in that it is certain to improve any situation. It is unpredictable in that we have no idea how or to what extent he intends to improve things.

Every one of us wants a great catch like the disciples got that day. The older I get, the fewer things I know for certain, but this is something I am sure of. We are all yearning for that type of catch in some area of our lives. Your need and yearning may be different than mine. You may be yearning for a great catch in your marriage. You may be yearning for a great catch in the area of health, personal finances, or career. You may be yearning for a baby, to overcome an addiction, or to belong to a more dynamic community. Whatever it is, we all have a yearning that is above all others, that is for good, that often seems impossible despite all our human efforts, that seems to require divine intervention of some type.

Every one of us wants a great catch like those fishermen got that day. But we often overlook the simplest and most vital truths. You don't get a catch like that in the shallow water. If you want that kind of a catch, you need to get out into the deep water and let down your nets. This is why in the spiritual life we are continually invited into deeper places, even as the world seems to be luring us into ever-shallower experiences of life and each other.

It is in the deep places that we are finally able to contemplate life, ourselves, and God, and all three are worthy of contemplation. To contemplate is to reflect upon something with depth and at length. Spending time in the deep places with God allows us to focus our hearts, minds, and souls on the things that matter most. What we think about, reflect upon, and contemplate, has an enormous impact on the events of our lives and the state of our souls. Paul counsels us, "Whatever is true, whatever is honorable, whatever is just, whatever is pure, whatever is pleasing, whatever is commendable, if there is any excellence and if there is anything worthy of praise, think about these things (Philippians 4:8)." Rushing here and there, throughout the course of our busy days, does not give us time to reflect on these higher things. The majority of messages the world shares with us lead us away from these higher things. For these and all the many other reasons we have discussed, God beckons us to spend a portion of our day with him contemplating the higher things.

Don't be afraid of the deep waters of the spiritual life. It is there that the most amazing experiences await you.

## THE DELIGHT OF GOD

Children desire to delight their parents. From a very early age, children are incredibly attentive to what it is that brings delight to their parents. It is therefore very important that parents choose carefully what they allow themselves to be delighted by in their children. Will we delight in how our children look, what they accomplish, or simply in who they are? This is one of the most powerful ways parents teach children what matters most, and in doing so set them on the right or wrong paths.

God delights in one thing above all else, and his delight teaches us some very powerful lessons.

My daughter, Isabel, wandered wistfully into my study the other day. As casually as she appeared and made herself comfortable on the couch, folding her feet underneath her, I sensed she wanted to talk. These are the things you become attuned to as a father, I suppose.

I set aside my work and settled into my place next to her on the couch. "How are you, baby?" I asked.

"Good," she said with her ever-buoyant tone and optimistic smile.

Isabel is eight, but her heart, mind, and soul already have the intricacies of a woman's. I see her mind at work; I notice the slightest joy and sadness cross her face and settle in her heart, and I get to witness her growing into her soul, embracing who she truly is and warding off the temptation to be less than who she was created to be. These are privileges and wonders that defy description.

Sitting there on the couch, I asked her a couple more questions: "How was school?" "What was the best thing that happened today?" "Do you have any problems you want to talk through with Daddy? Any questions you want to ask me?" Little by little, like a blossoming flower, she began to open up and talk. I knew she had come in to talk about something, but I sensed she was hesitant.

The conversation ebbed and flowed, before finally settling on what she had come in to talk about. I will not share the details of that conversation, but it is a thing of beauty to see your children concern themselves with things that are good and noble.

She talked for a few minutes and I listened. My beautiful girl just needed some reassurance. As she talked it through, I could see that she knew what she needed to do. "What is your heart telling you, baby?" I asked.

She knew, and I assured her that she knew. I could see a weight begin to lift from her little shoulders. Reassured, she began to move the conversation in a new direction. "So, how was your day, Daddy?" I walked her through my day, highlighting a couple of great things that had happened and pointing out a couple of tough decisions I'd had to make. I wish everyone in my life listened to me so attentively. I knew in the coming days she would ask me how some of these situations had unfolded; she was thoughtful like that.

The conversation then came to a natural pause. She untangled her legs, stepped toward me, wrapped her ever-lengthening arms around my neck, and hugged me for a long time, cuddling me the way a koala wraps its arms around a eucalyptus tree and rests its head on the trunk of the tree. I sat there thinking I was the luckiest man in the world. Lifting her head from my chest, she kissed me, and disappeared as quickly and quietly as she had appeared.

I didn't move. I just sat there in the quiet, allowing the moment to sink in and take full effect. My joy was over-flowing, and I whispered a prayer of gratitude, and then a prayer of hope. I was grateful she felt comfortable coming to speak to me, and hoping she would always feel comfortable doing so.

Then my mind wandered simultaneously in two directions. Two ideas. The first was from the Eliot Morris song "Anywhere with You." The lyrics that my mind settled on were, "You know that it's true. Perfect is anywhere with you." The second direction my mind went was toward the Bible. In chapter eight of Proverbs, King Solomon wrote about creation and wisdom, and how God delights in simply being with his sons and daughters.

What is the one thing that God delights in above all else? Simply being with you. The delight of God is to be with his sons and daughters.

In any great relationship there is a time to talk about the ordinary things that occupy our days, a time to speak about more serious matters—decisions to be made and issues that weigh heavy on our hearts—and a time simply to be together. This wordless togetherness happens at the height of intimacy. There is no longer any need for ego or persona, no need to explain ourselves, and no need to understand or be understood. All that is set aside as we immerse ourselves in a great pool of acceptance.

God delights in you. He delights in just being with you. When we invite him into our lives he dances for joy. It helps to have tools and techniques to get us started in our journey of prayer, but ultimately, we have no need of artificial methods and complex systems. We are his children. Just talk to him and be with him. He is your Father and he loves you.

## BUSY IS NOT YOUR FRIEND

From time to time, it is good for us to ask ourselves, "Is my life working?" It's a question I have asked myself many times throughout my life, and more than once the answer has been no. But I have never been sorry that I stumbled upon the question and found the courage to explore it.

Every time I have been nudged and realized my life wasn't working, being too busy has been part of the problem. Busy is not our friend. It makes us feel overwhelmed, tired, and inadequate. If busy were a person, would you spend all day with that person today, and then all day with that person again tomorrow? Busy is not your friend. This is a lesson I have had to learn too many times in my life. I fall into the common trap of overscheduling and overcommitting myself, and it usually happens when I am neglecting my daily habit of prayer.

We are taught to judge a tree by its fruits, and the fruits of busy are not good. Busy leads to overwhelmed, weary, tired, burned out, worn out, discouraged, anxious, and stressed. Which of these fruits do you want in your life?

Being overwhelmed is one of the most common feelings people experience today. When asked, "What one word would you use to describe how you feel on a daily basis?" too many people say *overwhelmed*.

How often do you feel overwhelmed? Do you feel like there is more to do than hours in the day? Are you overwhelmed with really important matters or things that are shallow and insignificant? Feeling overwhelmed is one of the most common emotions in society today. When we are preoccupied with things we do not believe to be the most important things in life, we become resentful. So it's not just that we are busy, but that we are busy with the wrong things. When we are busy with the right things, we are less likely to feel overwhelmed, and we can push through that for a short period knowing that we are doing the right things for the right reasons.

Busyness may be the main obstacle between God and his people in the modern world. The devil likes us to think that the main obstacles between us and God are all types of spectacular sins, but the devil prefers the unstated daily distraction of busy. Overwhelmed is the symptom, and focusing on the symptom won't cure the disease. The disease is busy.

Busy leads to overwhelmed, and overwhelmed leads to

weary. We all know the feeling of exhaustion at the end of a day when you have worked hard on the right things. There is great satisfaction in that tiredness. But we also know the exhaustion that comes from doing lots of nothing important. This exhaustion is heavy and draining. It is the exhaustion of the weary, and God did not create us to be weary.

Weary is a sure sign that God is not in these plans. "Come to me, all you who are weary and burdened," Jesus says, "and I will give you rest. Take my yoke upon you and learn from me, for I am gentle and humble of heart, and you will find rest for your souls. For my yoke is easy and my burden is light" (Matthew 11:28–30).

Are you weary? Tired? Burned out? Worn out? Overwhelmed? The bad fruit of busy just keeps piling up. Busy leads to overwhelmed, overwhelmed leads to weary, and weary leads to discouraged. Discouraged is another sure sign that God is far from our plans. And yet, it is also among the most common emotions in society today.

The daily habit of prayer gives us an opportunity to consider and regulate commitments before we agree to them. Sitting with God in the classroom of silence we can explore why we feel called or compelled to agree to add something to our schedule? What are our reasons and motives? Do we have a great desire to do it? Do we feel called by God to do it? Or do we feel pressured by family and friends or other external forces?

There are two techniques that I employ to gain clarity.

The first is to ask myself: Do I feel free to say no? If we are not free to say no, we are not free to say yes. The other involves transporting myself in my mind to the day of the commitment I am considering. Then I ask: How will I feel on the way to this commitment? We often find ourselves getting ready for something we have agreed to months ago and wondering why we said yes. How will I feel while I am at this meeting, event, party, etc.? We often find ourselves in the middle of a meeting wondering why we ever agreed to it in the first place. Finally, I ask myself: How will I feel on my way home? Sometimes we leave a commitment thinking that was a great use of time. On these occasions we feel satisfied and fulfilled. But sometimes we leave an event, meeting, gathering, regretful that we agreed to participate. On these occasions we tend to think that we have wasted time that could have been used much more discerningly. Our mind can easily go then to all the things we have on our to-do lists, and this can lead to feeling overwhelmed.

Prayer teaches us how to live by showing us what matters most and what matters least. It helps us to discern the true priorities of our lives and align our daily schedule with our discerned priorities. Daily prayer is a great opportunity to decide what commitments to agree to and which ones we are going to graciously decline.

You may also find it useful to sit with God and go through your current commitments. Take an inventory of your obligations. Are they life-giving to you and others? Are they essential? Are they self-imposed? When you agreed to them did you feel free to say no? If not, why not? This is a very practical and powerful way to spend some time in conversation with God.

From time to time, we all need to step back from who we are, where we are, and what we are doing, and take another look at ourselves. To live deeply and deliberately with focused intention, we need to assess the content of our lives. What's helping? What's hurting? Who is helping? Who is hurting? What do you know that you are pretending not to know? Does your life make sense to you? Is this the life you want? The life-changing habit of daily prayer helps us to make these assessments and so much more.

Over time the daily habit of prayer helps us to develop a deep unwavering peace about who we are, where we are, and what we are doing. It helps us to realize how few things really matter in the grand scheme of things – and there is actually a grand scheme of things.

Prayer is the antidote for the poison of busyness. It is by establishing a habit of daily prayer that we get clear about what matters most and what matters least. It helps us to gradually discover who we are and the meaning and purpose of our lives. Prayer inspires us to live with great intention and avoid wasting our lives. Busy drags our lives out of focus. Prayer brings our lives into focus.

You are where you are right now for a reason. So let me ask you, have you ever really tried prayer as a central component of your life? Sure, we have all dabbled in it from time to time. But have you ever given it a real place in your life? If you have, great. Are you willing to take it to the next level? If you haven't, are you willing to try placing prayer at the center of your days? Either way, you have a decision to make. Choose carefully. It is one of the biggest decisions you will ever make.

## SOUL NOTE:

*Soul,*
*Until you discover God's playfulness*
*you will not enter into the depths of the spiritual life.*
*Until you discover the playfulness of the child within,*
*you will not discover the playfulness of God.*
*Dance in the rain, play in the mud, lose track of time,*
*and maybe then you will find yourself lost in God,*
*and found once and for all.*

# Do You Hear That?

## DO YOU HEAR THAT?

It is the laughter of Rachel, Esther, Delilah, and Ruth;

It is David and Solomon laughing from deep in their bellies;

It is Jesus and his disciples laughing on the road from Jericho to Jerusalem;

It is Joseph laughing for joy when he discovered the golden nature of his dreams.

That sound you hear, it's the laughter of your unborn child;

It's your great-great-granddaughter laughing a hundred years from now;

It's your own unrestrained and unedited laugh set free for all to hear.

It is the laugh of 107 billion people, the laugh of forty thousand years, the laugh of eternity.

Listen carefully to life and closely to your heart,

and you will hear God laugh.

Sing with him, dance with him, laugh with him, cry with him, and love with him.

Everything is better with him!

I hope you have enjoyed

# I Heard God Laugh

It has been a great privilege to write for you.
May God bless you with a prayerful spirit
and a peaceful heart.


*Matthew Kelly*